savvy $AVING

melissa jennings & shelley king

hegemony press
an imprint of cedar fort, inc.
springville, utah

ISBN 13: 978-1-59955-952-0

Published by Hegemony Press, an imprint of Cedar Fort, Inc.
2373 W. 700 S., Springville, UT 84663
Distributed by Cedar Fort, Inc., www.cedarfort.com

LIBRARY OF CONGRESS CATALOGING-IN-PUBLICATION DATA

Jennings, Melissa, author.
  Savvy saving : couponing secrets from the stockpiling moms / Melissa Jennings, Shelley King Steimer.
    pages cm
  ISBN 978-1-59955-952-0
  1. Shopping. 2. Coupons (Retail trade) 3. Consumer education. I. Steimer, Shelley King, author. II. Title.

  TX335.J46 2011
  640.73--dc23

                              2011033191

Cover design by Danie Romrell
Cover design © 2012 by Lyle Mortimer
Edited and typeset by Kelley Konzak

Printed in the United States of America

10 9 8 7 6 5 4 3 2 1

Printed on acid-free paper

authors' note

Please refer to the glossary at the end of the book for useful abbreviations and helpful terms to know. You can also email us at info@stockpilingmoms.com for more information.

For more information from the Stockpiling Moms, please visit these great sites:

http://www.stockpilingmoms.com

http://www.cookingwithstockpilingmoms.com

http://www.melissa-jennings.com

http://www.shelley-king.com

contents

acknowledgments

This book is dedicated to our children, Peyton, Chase, and Caleb. You are the reason that we started stockpiling, so that we could stay home and be the mommies we always dreamed of. Thanks for always making us smile and for shopping with us more than you ever wanted to.

To our loving husbands, thanks for your support and dedication. Special thanks to Melissa's husband, Tim, who helped in the editing process and for being the best (unpaid) bookkeeper.

To our parents, thanks for your unwavering support and dedication. You are the best cheerleaders and role models, and without you, we would not be where we are today.

To our publisher and editor, thanks for your time and attention to detail.

To our readers, thanks for your continued support and for reading all of our posts. We appreciate you more than you will ever know. We can honestly say that we do it all for you. Thanks for following us and allowing us to help you save.

introduction

Stockpiling Moms.com is a family-friendly blog dedicated to helping families save money and stretch their budgets. Stockpiling Moms features deals, frugal recipes, menu planning, giveaways, frugal family-fun activities, and topics that make household management easier. In this book, the founders of Stockpiling Moms will share with you their journey to frugal living and strategies to save your family budget thousands of dollars a year by skillfully using coupons to build a stockpile.

In 2009, Melissa Jennings and Shelley King founded Stockpiling Moms.com and made it their mission to save money for their families. Through this book, they share how you can apply stockpiling to all aspects of your life to expand saving money to more than groceries. Melissa and Shelley are best friends who met through International Adoption. They have three boys, who were born in Guatemala. As stay-at-home moms for six years, they know what it takes to live a frugal lifestyle and to live within a budget.

They are stockpiling experts who want to help you stretch your family budget. Melissa taught family and consumer science (home economics) on the high school level for eleven years and holds a masters degree in education. By strategically using coupons, Melissa spends an average of 130 dollars a month on all her groceries (including organic milk, eggs, fruits, and vegetables), household products, and health and beauty aids for her family of three. Shelley spent three years as a substance abuse counselor, educating people and giving them the tools to aid them in living a healthy lifestyle. Shelley spends 300 dollars a month on all her groceries, household products, and health and beauty aids for her family, which includes one child in diapers and one in overnights. By mastering the art of using coupons, they are able to save thousands of dollars a year.

Since Melissa began stockpiling, she has been able to save over $15,000 from her family's grocery budget. It has been life changing! Shelley has saved approximately $10,000 from her family's grocery budget. Melissa and Shelley's goal is to save 50–100 percent every time they shop! Not only do they stockpile groceries, household items, and health and beauty aids, they also stockpile in every other aspect of their lives. In this book, they will share with you how to stockpile for the holidays, use coupons to eat healthy, apply strategies for living naturally frugal, save for your dream vacation, and skillfully use coupons to save between 50 and 70 percent every time you shop. Join Stockpiling Moms on the journey to frugal living. From this point, Stockpiling Moms will be referred to as "we" unless referring to either Melissa or Shelley individually.

Top 10 Reasons to Stockpile

10. You never have to pay full price for your gas again.

9. You can never have enough (free) cleaning products from your grocery's half-price sale!

8. With the hundreds of dollars you save a month, you can make a car payment, buy season passes to the zoo, afford extras for your children, or go on a date night!

7. You have enough free personal hygiene products for everyone in your neighborhood!

6. You are always prepared to whip up a recipe when unexpected company comes over for dinner.

5. You always have the ingredients on hand when your husband comes home and says, "I forgot to tell you we are supposed to bring in a dessert tomorrow."

4. When the weatherman predicts snow, you don't have to make a run for the grocery store.

3. You are always prepared in case of a natural disaster.

2. You never have to pay retail for your groceries.

1. With all the money you save from stockpiling, you can take your family on a dream vacation!

1

stockpiling 101

Let's start with the basics. A stockpile is a pile or storage location for bulk materials, including groceries and personal care or household products. In most cases when you refer to stockpiling, these are the items included; however, a stockpile can also include other items, as we will explain later in the book. You can easily extend the idea of stockpiling to all areas of your life to save money, which we do.

We want to start by introducing the concept of stockpiling to you. The concept of stockpiling is normally a major change in the way you currently shop. You are no longer going to make a grocery list for what you need at the store on a weekly basis. Instead you are going to shop for what you will use in longer terms. You are going to start shopping for what you will use in a three-month period of time—or longer, depending on the shelf life of the items on your list. Some items like health and beauty aids and household items won't expire for a year or two, so you can stockpile those items for a longer period of time, depending on the amount of storage that you have available.

When you stockpile your groceries by using coupons, you do not pay full price or retail for your groceries. Instead, your goal is to purchase them at the very lowest price, or what we call "rock bottom." We like to think of rock bottom being at least 70 percent off. Once you establish your stockpile, you are going to be able to really see

Tip:

Don't use a coupon just because you have it. Wait for the best deals and you'll save more!

the savings month after month. The longer you stockpile, the more you save. If you stockpile successfully, you will save hundreds of dollars every month, which equals thousands of dollars a year! Eventually you will no longer shop weekly from the store but instead shop weekly from your stockpile.

The objective is to "match" grocery sale prices to available coupons to take advantage of when prices are at rock bottom. By watching the sales cycle, you will know when the price is at rock bottom. Our number one stockpiling tip is do not use a coupon just because you have it. Clip your coupons today and use them strategically later. For example, if you find a good deal this week using your coupons but the products are not at rock bottom, you are going to wait to use your coupons because of the possibility that a better deal will come along before the coupon expires. Holding onto your coupons to use them at the lowest price is a strategic game of chance. There is no guarantee that a better deal will come along; however, you are also chancing that you will find the best deal possible at a stockpile price.

This is a sample shopping list to use:

Shopping List				
Item	Price	Coupon	Incentives Earned	Total OOP
Milk	$1.99	N/A	N/A	$1.99
Tide	$5.99	$1/1 (05/31 P&G)	$2 OYNO Catalina	$4.99

Our next stockpiling tip is never go to the store without a shopping plan. If you walk into the store without a plan, you will not walk out of the door with major savings. Every week, you should target what is free or nearly free. Then you should target what is at rock bottom and "match" what coupons you have. These are the items that you should stockpile. We have a weekly post at Stockpiling Moms.com each Tuesday called "Stockpile Time: Hot Steals & Deals at the Store," and we tell you exactly which items to stockpile every week. However, by watching your stores' sales cycles and matching coupons to sales, you will be able to figure out what and when to stockpile.

All coupon policies vary by store, so it is important to become familiar with your stores' coupon policies. Contact your local store manager or customer service desk and ask for the coupon policy in writing. You may find it available on the company website if there is a corporate policy. If it is available, you should place a copy into your coupon binder. This will come in handy if you encounter a cashier that doesn't know the policies as well as you do.

Finally, you "match" your coupons to the sales ads and purchase when you find a deal that is at "rock bottom." When you find the rock bottom deal, you want to stockpile or purchase the quantity necessary to last your family through the sales cycle. This can be tricky because some products like cereal cycle every six weeks but some products like baking goods or barbecue items only cycle at rock bottom once or twice a year.

We often get asked, "when is the right time to stockpile?" It is hard to teach a person "when" because the answer is when the price is at rock bottom. Rock bottom means 50–70 percent off, depending on where you live (in the land of doubles, the amount you save will be larger). The best way to figure out rock bottom is to watch how the products cycle in your area. There is no right price for rock bottom. Every region has different pricing, so what is important is to track the prices for your area. By watching the prices, you will begin to see the cycle and figure out when you should stockpile.

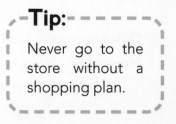

Tip:

Never go to the store without a shopping plan.

Our next stockpiling tip is to think logically when it comes to understanding the sales cycle. Products normally hit rock bottom at the time of year they will be used or right before that season starts. When an item is at rock bottom, this is when you want to match an available coupon to the sale price. If you decide to purchase your coupons (through coupon clipping services, where you pay for the time they spend clipping coupons, or by purchasing the Sunday paper to get coupons), we advise you to do so when they become available in the hopes that you will find a great sale in the future because coupons are often hard to purchase the week the deal becomes available.

In the past, products have cycled like this:

January: After Christmas Items, Towels, Linens, Oranges, Tangelos, Split Peas

February: Sodas, Chips, Snacks, Crackers, Cabbage, Potatoes, Onions

March: Allergy Items, Kleenex, Broccoli, Dried Beans, Grapefruit

April: Ham, Eggs, Baking Ingredients, Salsa, Corn Chips, Refried Beans, Carrots, Frozen Orange Juice, Greens

May: Asparagus, Eggs, Bananas

May and June: Barbecue Sauce, Marinades, Condiments, Country Time Lemonade, Charcoal, Hot Dogs, Dairy

June: Chicken, Strawberries, Dairy Products

July: Toys, Green Beans, Squash, Peaches

July and August: Back to School Supplies

August: Corn, Watermelon, Tomatoes

September: School Lunch Supplies, Capri Suns, Pop Tarts, Cabbage, Grapes, Pears

October: Apples, Cauliflower, Pork

November: Cough Medicine, Cold Medicine, Soup (Campbell's), Jell-O, Oats (Quaker), Tissues, Cranberries, Turkey, Turnips, Squash

December: Carnation Milk, Baking Ingredients, Wet Wipes, Boxed Stuffing and Potatoes, Canned Vegetables, Frozen Orange Juice, Potatoes, Tangerines

Also, some products like toilet paper, paper towels, soft drinks, and cereal cycle every 6–8 weeks. You want to watch the brands you use and purchase them when they are at their lowest price in the cycle. Hopefully you have a coupon to match, and when you do, it's stockpile time! If you don't have a coupon to match, it is still the time to purchase when the product is on sale. So by simply watching the sales cycle, you can save money from your grocery budget even without matching coupons. However, by matching coupons, you will be able to take your savings to another level.

For example, the following are stockpile prices for us:

Cereal: $1 per box or less

Oats: $0.50 per container or less

Cookie, Brownie, or Muffin Mix: $0.20 each or less

Mustard: $0.30 each or less

Barbecue Sauce: Free

Crackers: $0.50 per box or less

Fruit Snacks: $0.50 per box or less

Pancake Mix: $0.50 per box or less

Juice: $0.50 each or less

Milk: $1.25 per half gallon

Hand Soap: $0.30 each or less

Dishwasher Detergent: $0.50 each or less

Cleaning Supplies: $0.50 each or less

Deodorant: Free

Toothpaste: Free

Dental Floss: Free

Razors: Free

Shampoo: Free

Shaving Cream: Free

Body Wash: Free

Another great way to figure out when to stockpile is by creating a price book. A price book is simply a list of the products that you purchase on a regular basis and the price they cost each week. If you keep a price book, you will know when to stockpile because you will see how the prices cycle each week and when they are at a high and a low. You can create a price book using an excel spreadsheet easily, or, if you are like us, you like to have it with you in the store. We like to carry a hard copy of our list and then key it into our spreadsheet for tracking as well. A great way to keep it is in a notebook in your purse or in your coupon binder. We suggest setting it up either alphabetically or by categories for each store. Be sure to include the products you use on a weekly basis like eggs, milk, and bread as well as all items that you stockpile.

Here is a sample price book to use:

Price Book				
Store:				
Date	Product	Unit Size	Total Price	Price/Unit
6/19/2011	ex. Tylenol	150	$5.99	$0.04

It takes time to build a stockpile. We suggest taking three months (or more) to build a good stockpile that will last your family 3–6 months or more depending on the shelf life of the products. Normally, the first month, you will see an increase in your spending. As you are building your stockpile, this is normal because you have to continue to shop for what you need on a weekly basis while you are also stockpiling. By the end of the second and third months, you will begin to see major savings. At your fourth month, you will be saving hundreds of dollars a month.

We want to mention that it is normal to feel overwhelmed when you start building your stockpile. You may feel that you are at the grocery store more than you are not. You may be thinking, eating, breathing, and sleeping coupons. In fact, you may feel "coupon crazed." This is normal, and after the first several months, things will slow down. Our advice is to take your time and enjoy the savings, and it will be more enjoyable. It is normal to spend 20 hours a week when you first start this process. Just remember, if you don't have that amount of time to devote, you can spend less and just take longer to build your stockpile. However, for most people, once they start saving, they never look back. After you have built your stockpile, it is normal to spend four to five hours weekly to maintain it. This includes time clipping and organizing your binder. Another stockpile tip is that you don't have to get in on every deal, and remember, most deals eventually come back around. We suggest setting a budget for your grocery spending. We will discuss this later in the book.

Your ultimate goal is to save 50–70 percent of your current spending. For example, before Melissa started stockpiling, she was spending $450–$500 a month to feed her family of three. Now she is spending on average $130 month to feed her family. Shelley has two children in diapers or pull-ups. She was spending $600 a month to feed her family of four, and now she is spending on average $300 a month to feed them. As you can see, by stockpiling, they are able to save 50–70 percent from their budget each month. The bottom line is that whatever you are currently spending can be cut in half or more by utilizing these stockpiling strategies. Depending on your stores' coupon policies and the incentives they offer, you may be able to save up to 70 percent or even more!

There are many reasons we stockpile. The number one reason is to save our family money, but there is another reason. We like the feeling of knowing that our family is able to survive in case of an emergency. We know that our family could survive for at least six months, if not longer, with the items we currently have stockpiled.

Feeling confident that your family would be able to survive in the case of a disaster or emergency, whether that is a natural disaster or a job loss, gives you significant peace of mind. We are not including this to scare you but rather to make you aware that stockpiling has another benefit for your family in addition to saving money. You should be prepared for your family in case of a crisis, loss of employment, natural disaster, or other emergency. As Melissa's mom says, "It is better to be prepared."

Every family's stockpile will be different, based on what that family eats and uses. We both try to have on hand at any given time twenty or more boxes of cereal, for example. In addition to our stockpile, at any given time we have five gallons of milk, ten loaves of bread, five half gallons of orange juice, and several cartons of eggs frozen in our deep freezer. However, this may or may not be enough to last your family through a three-month period. We do suggest stockpiling bottled water if you want to prepare your stockpile for emergency situations. In addition to stockpiling groceries, you should also stockpile over-the-counter drugs, health and beauty aids, and household items that your family would need if there were a natural disaster or health-related outbreak. Of course, don't stockpile a quantity larger than what your family can use before the expiration date or you will not save money but rather waste it.

We suggest making a list of items that you use on a regular basis because these are items to target when you build your stockpile.

Items to stockpile may include but are not limited to

Toilet Paper	Medicine	Makeup
Dishwasher Detergent	Cleaning Products	Laundry Detergent
Soap	Shave Gel	Face Wash
Razors	Shower Gel	Paper Towels
Deodorant	Sponges	Pet Supplies
Conditioner	Shampoo	Water

Snacks	Canned Goods	Cereal
Soda	Styling Products	Toothpaste
Toothbrushes	Mouthwash	Resealable Bags
Pop-Tarts	Frozen Foods	Gum

Basic Terms

There are basic terms that you need to know in order to strategically use coupons. The first that we want to share with you is "overage." **Overage** is when you purchase an item for $0.80 and use a coupon for $1. At some stores, you will get the $0.20 back to be used toward another item in your order. We never count on overage when couponing unless it is written into the store coupon policy, but we love it when we get it! You *normally do not* get cash back, although sometimes you will, based on the store's coupon policy. If you won't receive actual cash back, then you will want to purchase another item so that the "overage" applies toward that item in your grocery cart. We suggest placing items in your cart like perishables that often don't have coupons. Overage is how we reduce the cost of our perishables. If your store will give you cash back, then you can use that money to purchase additional groceries at that store or even at another store.

Another way to get overage is when you "stack" coupons. **Stacking** coupons is using both a manufacturer and a store coupon on the same product at the same time. If a store allows you to stack, this is a great way to get additional savings. Some stores will let you use a manufacturer coupon and a store coupon at the same time on one product. The manufacturer pays for one coupon, and the store pays for the other. Oftentimes, this makes a product free after the coupon or may even be a moneymaker by giving you overage on the product. This is a great way to purchase additional items, using the overage to pay for them, which again reduces your out-of-pocket expense.

Some stores allow stacking with digital coupons too. This is an additional way to increase your savings. The ability to stack digital coupons with paper coupons will vary based on the store's coupon policy, so it is important to check with your store to see what their coupon policy is. There are often specific guidelines in regard to how and when coupons can stack, so it is important for you to read your store's policy before you shop. If a store allows you to stack digital coupons, then you can use one paper coupon and one digital coupon on the same item, similar to stacking a store coupon with a manufacturer coupon.

Oftentimes, by carefully using two coupons—whether a combination of a digital, store, or manufacturer coupon—on the same product, you will not only net a free product but may also earn overage. This is referred to as a **moneymaker**. Some stores automatically adjust your coupon down to match the item's sale price, and other stores give you the face value of the coupon. You don't have to feel guilty in earning overage because the manufacturer pays the store for the face value of the coupon regardless of how much you purchased the product for. The store also makes a handling fee for processing each coupon.

Please don't allow a cashier to make you feel bad for getting items for free. Oftentimes, cashiers do not understand overage and will make rude comments to you while you are checking out. They may say that you are stealing from the store. You are not stealing from the store by adeptly using coupons. You can take time to politely educate the cashier that what you are doing is legal or you can ignore the comments. We will talk about carefully selecting your cashier later in the book. As long as you're not fraudulently using coupons, you have no reason for concern.

Your coupon may "beep" when you use it. This does not mean that it is being used fraudulently. Often coupons beep because of the way they are coded into the cash register. If a product is priced less than the value of the coupon, it will often beep. Once, when shopping, Melissa used a coupon that beeped, and she had to explain to the cashier that she could either use the coupon for the face value or she could adjust it down to match the product price. The cashier did not believe Melissa and went over to a customer service manager, and the customer service manager told her that Melissa was correct.

For this example, Melissa "made" a total of $0.06 in overage on the item. The store did not give Melissa the $0.06 back in the form of cash, but it applied the money to another item in her cart. We just want you to be aware that if a coupon beeps, it does not mean that you are using it incorrectly. However, if a coupon beeps, the cashier will have to manually override it, and some cashiers might not do that.

For us, overage is a cherry on top of a sundae! We don't always count on it, but we love it when we get it! It is a nice way to save additional money while couponing and to get savings toward other items in your cart for which coupons aren't often offered, like meat, dairy, eggs, and produce. This is a great way to take your savings to another level. To find out if your store allows overage, consult your store's coupon policy. We do find that oftentimes overage will vary based on your cashier. However, if a store policy allows overage, be sure that the cashier is giving it to you. This can make a huge difference in your savings.

Another term to know is **rain checks**. We can't count the number of times we have gone to the store to find out that the "hot item" we wanted was out of stock. With the large number of couponers out shopping (and that number is increasing daily), utilizing rain checks is a useful tool when it comes to stockpiling. A rain check will allow you to purchase the out-of-stock item at a later date for the current sale price. By obtaining a rain check, you are able to get in on the sale after the store restocks the item, even if that is after the sale has ended. Rain checks can be useful instead of going back and forth to the store daily to see if the item has been restocked.

Depending on what store you are requesting a rain check from, the process will vary. Some employees will actually check inventory. Others will ask to see the ad with the price printed so they can verify, and some just take your word for it. It also varies by store as to where you will request a rain check. At some stores, you request rain checks at the service desk and they are handwritten. At other stores, they are printed on receipt paper and can be requested at either the checkout or the service desk. At CVS, they can be requested at checkout and are handwritten, and what is wonderful about CVS rain checks is that they have no expiration date! Stores that write rain checks include Kroger, CVS, Walgreens, Target, and Meijer. Always look at your store coupon policy or ask customer service to see if they issue rain checks. At most stores, in order to get a rain check, the item must be printed in the sales circular. It cannot be an unadvertised sale.

By asking for and using rain checks, you can have more stockpiling success than without them. We often hope for an item to be out of stock because it extends the sale price and allows us the opportunity to purchase additional coupons (if we want). The only time we are not hoping for a rain check is when we have a coupon that is expiring, and then a rain check won't benefit us without being able to match it to our coupon. If we are hoping for a rain check, we often go at the end of the sale. You must request a rain check in the week that a sale is running for it to be issued. You cannot request a rain check for an expired sales ad.

We mentioned that incentives are one of the keys to stockpiling success. One key incentive is the **Catalina**. Have you heard of using a CAT, or Catalina, and wondered if someone was talking about a pet or salad dressing? A Catalina is a manufacturer coupon dispensed at the register after a purchase. Catalinas are printed based on a purchase you make. Occasionally, if you make a purchase on a brand, you will get a "money off another brand" coupon: a Catalina. However, every week there are specific Catalina offers available at participating stores. If you make a qualifying purchase, where you purchase x of a particular brand in the same order, you will earn an "on your next order" Catalina. These are called OYNO (On Your Next Order) Catalinas. Not all stores dispense Catalinas. If your store does, there is a machine at the register that prints them after your purchase. They are printed like a receipt from their own machine beside the register when you check out. Be sure to always get your Catalinas, if they print, before you leave the store.

If you work Catalina offers to your favor, then often after coupons and Catalinas earned, many times your product will be free. Often the Catalinas "roll," meaning that when you do one transaction, you can use the Catalina for a second transaction so you are spending very little or nothing out of pocket. If a Catalina is not rolling, then when you pay with a Catalina coupon for the same item, another Catalina coupon will not print.

Always be sure that the Catalina machine is working properly before you check out. If it has a green light lit, then the machine is working correctly. If you have a problem with a Catalina not printing correctly, you can ask the customer service desk after you check out or call the Catalina Marketing toll-free number, (877) 210-1917, option 1.

Most Catalina coupons can only be redeemed at the store where the logo is imprinted. However, you can use competitor manufacturer Catalinas at some stores. Check your store's coupon policy to see if they accept competitor manufacturer coupons. If your store accepts competitor Catalina coupons, this can be useful to you to match with items that are on sale at a different store than the store that issued the Catalina. Also, note that since Catalinas are manufacturer coupons, they are treated as such in regard to wording in a coupon policy; that is you would look to see if your store accepts competitor manufacturer coupons.

That brings us to talk about double coupons. This is another key incentive to stockpiling success. We are often asked how we are able to save so much money at the store. The answer is simple, really: by masterfully using coupons and understanding the sales cycle. Regardless of where you live, if you start watching your sales cycle and create a price book, you will be able to see how prices cycle each week and stockpile when the prices are at rock bottom. After you have done this for a while, you will figure out when a product is at the lowest price during the cycle. Next you match any available coupons when the product is at rock bottom or the lowest price during the cycle, and that is when you should stockpile.

Now, with that being said, we live in the "land" of doubles. Our stores double coupons up to $1. So, for example, a coupon that has a face value of $0.25 doubles to $.50, a coupon with a face value of $0.50 doubles to $1, which is normal in many areas; however, in addition, coupons that have a value of $0.51–$0.99 double to $1 in value. Plus, our store doubles unlimited amounts of coupons! So this is what we call living in the "land" of doubles. Some stores even offer triple coupons; for example, from $0.25 to $0.75 or $0.50 to $1.50. Other stores double coupons $1 to $2. It is important for you to compare the coupon policies at all of the stores available to you and then make a decision on where to shop based on where you can utilize your coupons.

If a coupon's bar code starts out with a five, it will almost always double if you are using it at a store that doubles coupons, even if it states, "Do not double." However, if a coupon's bar code starts with a nine, it will not double unless the cashier forces it to. We are finding now, though, that many stores will not double a coupon if it says "Do not double," regardless of whether it starts with a five or a seven. This will vary based on your store's coupon policy. We find that store coupons and digital coupons generally do not double

However, we do want to mention that regardless of whether you live in the "land" of doubles or not, you can easily save up to 50 percent off of your groceries by strategically using coupons and matching coupons during the sales cycle. By living in the "land" of doubles, we are able to take our savings to 70 percent. There are ways that you can increase your savings, such as by submitting mail-in rebates and using monthly menu planning. You may have to think outside of the box to get higher savings, but it is possible. We will discuss these other ways to save later in the book.

We have been asked, "is it worth driving out of your town for a store that doubles or triples?" We really think you have to factor in the cost of gas and of your time. We personally don't think it is worth it to drive an hour or more to shop at a store that doubles or triples unless you find that your savings will justify it. If you do, then yes, we would consider it. If you are going to be in an area that doubles or triples and you could work in a shopping trip while there anyway, then yes, we would think that is worth it. However, it is best to plan your shopping trip before you go to the store.

Another strategy is **price matching**. Price matching is a great tool. If you are not familiar with price matching, what it means is that if your store allows it, you can get the same price a competitor store is offering for an item at a store that may be more conveniently located to you. We love to price match because it keeps us from driving all over town. A few stores do price match. One store that price matches is Walmart, who price matches with a current sales flyer. Some stores actually provide the current sales ads for you so that you don't have to provide them. In order to price match, the ad may not be printed off the internet; it must be an original sales curricular with a current date. When checking out, show the sales flyer to the cashier, and they will manually change the price down to match the competitor's price.

We really like to price match because it not only saves us time but also saves us money. We no longer have to drive to a store that is out of our way because we can price match at a store that we would be going to anyway. For example, one week a local store had avocados priced at $0.29. We simply took the sales ad to our local store that price matches and got it for the same price! Price matching can be a great tool. When making your shopping lists, consider price matching to save you time and money.

Price Match				
Item	Location	Price	Coupon	Total OOP
Milk	Walmart	$1.99	N/A	$1.99
Tide	Kroger	$5.99	$1/1 (05/31 P&G)	$4.99

Target price matches as well. If you find an item in a competitor's printed ad that is priced lower than it is at your Target store, they will match the price. The competitor's ad must be local and current, and the product must be the identical item, brand name, quantity, and model number. Competitor catalogs can also be ad matched as long as the catalog displays a valid date and meets all other qualifications. Target does not price match Target.com prices.

Another store that price matches is Kohl's. If you find the same item with a lower price at another store, they will match or beat the competitor's price. Just bring a copy of the competitor's ad with the current date on it to your nearest Kohl's department store. Make sure the ad includes a description of the item. This applies to in-store prices and products only, not to Kohls.com pricing or products. If you are not utilizing price matching, it is definitely a resource to consider.

Another term to know is "**unadvertised sales**." Every week, all stores offer unadvertised specials. While shopping, you want to keep your eyes peeled and walk up and down every single aisle looking for unadvertised sales and managers' specials. You can often find great markdowns on meat, dairy, and produce as well as clearance items. Unadvertised specials or managers' specials matched with coupons can often make these items free or close to free! Also, this is a great time to look for coupons and rebates at the store. We will discuss this later in the book.

Do you love the thrill from scoring a freebie? We do! After a great score at the store, there is nothing that gets our adrenaline pumping more than a great save. Do you know what we mean? You do if you have experienced it. We love saving 70 percent or more when we go to the store, and when we do, we leave the store feeling so good! We call it the "coupon high." As you begin the process of stockpiling, you are sure to get the rush from saving so much money at the store. With the thrill of couponing and saving money, you'll enjoy the "coupon high" too! When we started stockpiling, we would lay out our purchases and play the guessing game with our husbands, post pictures of our shopping successes on facebook, and really enjoy the "high." In fact, we still do.

Mail-in rebates (MIR) are an excellent avenue for taking your savings to the next level. Melissa normally submits an average of $75 in rebates each month. There are a variety of rebates that you can redeem. Many stores offer rebates, such as Bed, Bath & Beyond, Walgreens, Kohl's, Ace Hardware, Staples, Office Max, Toys R Us, and Rite Aid. The key to rebate success is to keep your eyes open when you are in the store and then submit the forms immediately. There are several benefits to submitting immediately. You will have less of a chance of losing a required item if you do, and you will begin the process for getting your out-of-pocket expense back once the rebate is filed.

Mail-in rebates are offered by manufacturers or stores. Offers can be found in-store, on a tear pad, online, or in the Sunday newspaper inserts. An additional source for rebates is by trade. We have used www.weusecoupons.com/upload /need-rebate for finding rebates. It is a great way to trade because you don't pay for the rebate, you just pay for the postage stamp to mail it to you. It is a great resource for finding additional rebates. In addition, you can trade rebates at StockpilingMoms.com.

Tip:

Stay organized by filing your receipts.

A lesser-known mail-in rebate is beer and wine rebates. These are found in stores by the product, at the customer service desk, or with the cashier (in a liquor store). Many states do not require the purchase of beer or wine. These rebates are often overlooked or unknown. The rebates are often for a specific item that you may be purchasing already, for example, meat and cheese trays, potato chips, hams, turkeys, charcoal, or grilling ingredients. Some stores also offer deli rebates. We always stop at the deli counter or customer service desk and inquire if they have any rebates available. A stockpiling tip is to check for hang tags on wine bottles and stop at your customer service desk and inquire if they have any beer rebates available. Oftentimes they keep them in a drawer by the cash register. We also always ask the "beer man" when we see him making deliveries too.

In order to maximize your rebates, you need to keep all of your receipts. We suggest keeping them for a minimum of three to six months. We have an accordion folder that we keep them in by month for six months. The great thing about rebates is that you never know when you will come across one that you can match to an item that you have already purchased. A stockpiling tip is to stay organized by filing receipts.

When this happens, you have an instant moneymaker! Speaking of moneymakers, when you use coupons to purchase items that you then submit for rebate, you can often make money on the items. In general, the majority of rebates are moneymakers. This is a great way to improve your savings. We like to match coupons to items that submit for rebate when possible.

It is crucial to keep up to date with your pending rebates. Not only do we keep a copy of every rebate form and the necessary documentation that we submit, we also keep a photocopy of the receipt. We date the original and then photocopy and file it in a "pending rebates" file folder. We record each rebate into an excel spreadsheet with the date, source, contact information, and amount of the rebate, as well as the date we receive the rebate. If we don't receive the rebate check in the time that the rebate allows, we then follow up with the status of the rebate. You may think this is a lot of work, but in the end, we gain an additional savings of on average $75 per month!

See one example here:

Product	Company	Submitted	Received	Amount

The Four Keys to Stockpiling Success

Store Loyalty—You are going to have to shop at a variety of stores in order to get in on the best deals. This may be a major change for you. If you are loyal to one store, you will not be able to get in on all the deals. You are going to need to compare the coupon policies at the stores in your area and shop at a variety of stores based on the deals that they offer. Some weeks we go to five stores to shop, other weeks we shop at only one store, and there are even weeks we don't shop at all. However, if you don't shop at a variety of stores, you will not be able to see the major savings. Evaluate the stores that you have available to you and their coupon policies to make this decision.

We suggest that you strategically plan your shopping trips. When you are planning your errands or will be in an area that has several stores in close proximity, plan your coupon run accordingly. We suggest placing a cooler in your trunk so that you can place your perishables inside and continue your errands. Start with the furthest store away and end with the store where you are purchasing frozen items or perishables. We try to plan so that we make no more than three stops at a different store in one trip. This is manageable for us. When starting out, it may be best to start with one store and build up. By planning errands and your shopping trips, you will save time and money.

Brand Loyalty—If you want to get in on the deals, then you can't be brand loyal. This is a major change and is hard for some people. We always bought the same brands, so when we started stockpiling, we had to open our mind to this type of shopping. If you open your mind, the savings are there for you to take advantage of. The manufacturers are providing coupons for us to use. Coupons are like cash, so using them is a great way to save big. However, you have to be willing to try new products to take advantage of the savings. Coupons are often for new products or brands that you may or may not use on a regular basis.

One example is that we had always purchased a certain brand of dishwasher detergent. When we started stockpiling, we kept hearing about cheap or free dishwasher detergent; however, it was a different brand than what we were familiar with. We decided we had nothing to lose and gave it a try. The brand we were regularly using released only a very small value coupon, versus the other brand, who had a nice, high-end value coupon. When the other brand netted to be free after the coupon, we decided we had nothing to lose. After trying the detergent, not only did we love it, we also realized being brand loyal was not all it was cracked up to be.

As another example of brand loyalty, our families always used a specific brand of peanut butter. When we started stockpiling, a store had a free peanut butter deal, but it was for a different brand of peanut butter than what we normally used. We decided to give it a try because we were not out any money to purchase the other brand, and in the end, our families liked the other brand better than our regular brand (maybe because it was free)! If you are willing to try new brands, you will be able to save big. So it was a great decision for us to try brands that we normally would not have tried. We suggest giving all brands a chance, especially if they are free or close to it!

Another stockpiling tip is that you may need to avoid store brands. Manufacturers provide coupons for us to use with their brands. We don't see store brand coupons as often, especially those that would net free in a sale. We suggest comparing the brand name product price after coupon to the store brand, and whichever product is less would be the one that you should purchase. Most often, we do not purchase the store brand but rather the brand name product. This brings us to talk about the next strategy.

Incentives—Factor in any incentives you have to shop at a store. There are many incentives to factor into your decision. Some stores double or triple coupons. Other stores offer "on your next order" coupons (Catalinas) when you make a qualifying purchase. Other stores, like Target, offer a gift card as an incentive when you make a qualifying purchase or overage. Always consider these incentives before you shop. They should be factored into your decision about where you will make your purchases to give you the best deals. We will discuss these incentives more later in the book.

Product Size—A big mistake that we used to make as a shopper was buying the biggest product size available. In the past, we have compared the unit price when buying the largest size, giving us the best price per unit (or so we thought). You are no longer going to buy the largest size available; in fact, you are going to purchase the smallest size allowable based on the wording on your coupon. This is a huge change for most shoppers. One product size may be less expensive per unit, but the smaller item may be free or close to free after your coupon. For example, if you buy paper towels in large packages (for example, a twelve-roll package), this limits you to use one coupon. However if you buy three, four-roll packages of paper towels, you are now going to be able to use three coupons, which will equate to more in savings, oftentimes even netting free or near free! It is very important to use your coupons on the smallest size allowable based on the wording of your coupon.

Taking this to another level, you could use a "$1 off any" coupon on a 26-oz. package of detergent or, because the wording says "any," you could use it on a travel size, possibly getting the package free, depending on the value of the coupon. This is an example of strategic coupon use. You will want to purchase products in the smallest size that your coupon allows. If a coupon doesn't have a size limit, then you can use it for travel size or the smallest size available and possibly get that product for free. This is a new way of shopping for most people because shopping by the unit price makes us think that buying the bigger product is the best deal, when in reality, purchasing the smallest size allowable matched with a coupon is often a much better deal.

Product size leads us to talk about buying in bulk. If you are going to prudently use coupons, there is no reason to shop at large warehouse stores. Most warehouse stores do not allow you to use coupons, and if they do, then they don't sell small product sizes. This brings us back to using a coupon strategically on the smallest size available instead of by the price per unit. If you are purchasing the smallest size available using coupons, you will do far better than purchasing large quantities without using coupons. There are a few products that do price better at a warehouse store, but in general, it may no longer be worth your membership if you are using coupons. Always check with the warehouse clubs to see what their coupon policy is and decide if it is worth maintaining your store membership. Whether the warehouse club accepts coupons would determine if it would be worthwhile to pay for a yearly membership.

There are three major wholesale clubs, BJ's, Costco, and Sam's Club. You have to pay a membership fee in order to shop at each. Unless you are shopping for a business or an organization, you typically would need only a basic membership. You should compare the stores that you have available to you and their coupon policies, if applicable, and factor in the cost to be a member.

BJ's accepts both store coupons and manufacturer coupons (they can be stacked). At BJ's, if you purchase a multipack of items, you can combine a store coupon and a manufacturer's coupon for each item in the multipack; this is a great tip to save big! For example, if you purchase a multipack of three boxes of razor blades, you could use a store and manufacturer coupon for each box of razor blades, if applicable. So if you have a BJ's in your area, this may be a good choice for you with regard to wholesale clubs.

Costco does not accept manufacturer coupons; however, they do distribute monthly store coupons to members. Sam's Club does not accept manufacturer coupons, and only premium members receive store coupons. By comparing the policies, you will be able to see if a membership is worthwhile to you. Remember that stores change their policies, so always check to see what the current coupon policy is.

For example, at Sam's Club you cannot use manufacturer coupons or store coupons with a regular membership. If you are using coupons purchasing the smallest size allowable based on the wording of your coupon, you will do far better using your coupons at a store that accepts coupons than purchasing large sizes without using coupons. Occasionally some products, like perishables, are priced lower at the wholesale club, so you should consider how much of those products you use. You should also factor in whether or not you get overage at the stores available to you to help offset the cost of your perishables.

Tip:

Shop the clearance section to save big!

If you decide to become a wholesale club member, you can "gap" your membership. When your membership is nearing expiration, stock up on items you need to last you three to six months. As you run low on these products, renew your membership. By doing this, you will pay the membership fees every fifteen to eighteen months versus every twelve. It is one way to save you some money when it comes to paying for the wholesale club membership fees. Another idea is to share a membership if the store allows. Both of these strategies help reduce the expense of becoming a member and may make it more worthwhile.

Another tip is to shop the clearance section. Each wholesale club offers product markdowns. These items may make for major savings and may price better than an item after coupon at the grocery store. But in many cases, it won't. Items to consider purchasing at wholesale clubs include perishables and items that you cannot find coupons for. In particular, dairy products, including milk, eggs, and butter don't often have coupons. By purchasing these items, you may be able to save enough to compensate for your membership cost. Some wholesale clubs offer discounts on prescriptions, gasoline, alcohol, gift cards, and photos. You could factor in these discounts if applicable when deciding if you want a membership.

At Costco, you can purchase gift cards to local and national restaurants and retailers for 20 percent off. This may be a worthwhile incentive to pay for your membership. Just remember purchasing some items in bulk may not really be a great deal if you don't use them. Consider shopping with a friend to split large containers so that they don't go bad before you use them or consider freezing to extend the shelf life.

The biggest thing to remember is that just because an item is sold in bulk does not mean it is a better price than purchasing the smaller size with a manufacturer coupon, especially if you can shop at a store that doubles. You should carry a calculator and create a price book when you shop so you can divide the total cost by the amount in the package and compare if you can purchase it for a lesser price at the grocery store using a coupon. Hopefully this helps you in deciding if a wholesale club membership is worthwhile to you.

2

collecting coupons

In order to successfully stockpile, you are going to need to purchase or obtain multiple newspapers that contain coupon inserts. Look for a newspaper that offers the SmartSource, Red-Plum, P&G, and General Mills inserts. In general, these inserts can be found in the Sunday newspaper. However, oftentimes, weekly newspapers will carry coupon inserts too. Check for a local paper deal in your area or see if your newspaper will offer a discount for ordering multiple papers. Often inserts are included in additional mailers, so always check your junk mail. A stockpiling tip is to look at your local dollar store. Oftentimes they are less expensive than other stores. We suggest purchasing your newspapers in increments of two to take advantage of BOGO sales at the store.

It is very important to preview the upcoming coupons each week at TaylorTownPreview.com or SundayCouponPreview.com so that you can determine how many papers you want to purchase each week. We post a Sunday Coupon Preview every week on Thursday at StockpilingMoms.com. This gives you an idea of which coupons will be in the Sunday newspaper. You should understand that the values and coupons can vary regionally. The preview gives you an idea of how many papers and what coupons you want to purchase each week; however, always check your local paper to see if there are any regional variations. A stockpiling tip, there are normally no coupon inserts in the newspaper on holiday weekends. We have many disappointed readers who have purchased large quantities of papers when starting out on a holiday weekend, so this is a really helpful stockpiling tip.

Another resource for collecting coupons is purchasing from a coupon clipping service. Instead of purchasing multiple papers for only one or two hot coupons that you want in a large quantity, you can order those coupons online through a coupon clipping service. When you purchase from a coupon clipping service, you are not paying for the coupon but rather for the time clipping it. You should never pay face value (or more) for a coupon. For example, if a coupon is $1/1 we would pay no more than $.10 for that coupon, to give you an idea. We suggest the following coupon clipping services: TheQHunter.com, KuntryKlippers.com, CouponBeat.com, and CouponDeDe.com. We like to use coupon clipping services because as busy moms, it is a huge time saver for us. It is also a way to be "green" in targeting specific coupons versus purchasing an additional newspaper. You can often purchase whole inserts in addition to clipped coupons. Another benefit is that this allows you to purchase coupons from other regions than your own. If your Sunday newspaper doesn't contain coupons, this is a good alternative as well.

Another resource is to ask people for their inserts or what is left after they clip their inserts. Simply put the word out to all of your friends, family, and neighbors that you are using coupons, and you will be amazed at how many people will share their coupons or what is left after they clip their coupons with you. You may even want to consider dumpster diving. This is when you look for inserts in a paper-only recycling bin. Though we have never done it, many of our readers have had great success. We suggest wearing rubber gloves and only grabbing what you can reach (not jumping into the dumpster). It is important to bring a box to collect your inserts too. Another resource to check into is craigslist.com or freecycle.org.

If you are purchasing several papers a week, you will find that you end up with many "extra" coupons. Consider organizing a coupon swap because it is a great way to exchange those extras for coupons you can use instead. We created an exchange when we started stockpiling with several of our friends. We got together once a week and simply swapped coupons while our children played. It was nice because we traded "leftover" coupons with each other and put them to use. We trade with neighbors, which is convenient and a great resource. It is easy to pass coupons between neighbors too. We simply pass them from house to house.

Another suggestion is to start a coupon swap at work or church. For those interested, place your leftover coupons into a container with a lid labeled "COUPONS," and then everyone can pass the container back and forth or you can simply place it in a public location. Consider forming a lunch bunch swap and enjoy a sack lunch together while you swap. Create a coupon swap with members of your MOMS Club, MOPS, Homemakers, or PTSO. Swap with the moms at your children's school; ask if you can swap in an extra room of the cafeteria after drop off or before pick up. Another idea is to email a group of friends and see who would be interested in participating and how often.

You could also join a coupon train. We have one at Stockpiling-Moms.com, and it is free to join. This is a group of people from all over the Unites States who mail an envelope of clipped coupons to each other. There is a "conductor," who organizes the train. There is normally a minimum of fifty coupons in the original envelope, and the conductor starts by mailing it to the next passenger on the list. That person removes as many coupons as they desire and replaces it with the same number of coupons from their supply that they are not going to use and then mails it to the next passenger. When a person receives the envelope, they must agree to replace the coupons and mail it out to the next person on the list within three days. Because coupons expire, it is important to mail it quickly. It is suggested to have one conductor and six passengers. The last passenger mails it back to the conductor, and then it starts again. Each passenger would also remove any expired coupons as the train travels and replace with current coupons. You can have general coupon trains or specific trains, for example, "pet" or "baby" coupon trains. This is a great way to exchange your coupons for ones from other regions.

Swapping is great because while you may not use baby coupons or pet coupons, those are in high demand for many others. It is easy to trade them for a brand that you do use, and that way they don't go to waste. If you form a diverse group, that will make swapping even more profitable! You don't have to have a large group to start. Swapping with just two to four people is a great way to get started.

Another great resource that is often overlooked is to collect coupons at the store. This is one of our favorite methods of collecting coupons. Collect blinkies, tear pads, and hang tags while you are shopping. These are coupons provided by the manufacturer and are always available for free in the store! Collect them while you shop and use them later when an item is on sale at rock bottom! However, do not remove peelies from packages in the store. They came into the stores attached to the package, and the manufacturer wants them to be used at the time of purchase. It is not ethical to remove peelies.

Asking your children to collect coupons at the store is a great way to get them involved, plus we find that they have great eyes for finding coupons that we may not see. We never take more than our fair share (a rule of thumb is to collect no more than one per family member) or all that are available. For example, if there are only two, we would take only one. Some people don't feel comfortable collecting coupons from the store; however, we have spoken to many store managers who have no problem with it at all. The coupons are available for the consumer, so you should not feel uncomfortable taking them. What is important is to not clear the store of coupons that you find.

You can print coupons from a variety of sources online. These are called Internet Printable coupons (IPs). Most IP coupon sites require you to install a coupon printer to your computer. This is because the coupon is attached to your IP address. This is a security measure to help with coupon fraud. You will have to be able to download and run the program in order to print. If you cannot install the coupon printer, you will not be able to print.

IPs have a printing limit set by the manufacturer and will run out of available prints. There is no way to know when they are close to their printing limit. We suggest printing them when they are released at the beginning of the month, especially high end or "hot" coupons. They often reset throughout the month as well. IPs can be printed in black and white or grayscale to save costs on colored ink cartridges. Another stockpiling tip is to take advantage of mail-in rebates for copy paper at office supply stores. You can often get reams of paper for free. Stores to consider are Staples, Office Depot, and Office Max. You can also look for ink rebate programs at office supply stores or purchase your ink online through 123inkjets.com.

You are also limited to how many coupons you can print per IP address. If you have access to more than one IP address, you can print more coupons! There are several sources for IPs, including Coupons.com, RedPlum.com, CoolSavings.com, SmartSource.com, CouponNetwork.com, and MamboSprouts.com. You can print your IPs at StockpilingMoms.com. IPs are sometimes harder to use because the cashier will need to confirm they are legitimate. Also, not all stores accept them (always check your store's coupon policy), and others are cautious about accepting IPs because many stores have dealt with coupon fraud in the past in regard to IPs. You should never photocopy or scan an internet coupon (or any coupon).

We have had cashiers hold IPs up to the light, feel them, and inspect them carefully. You never have anything to worry about, though, if you have not photocopied the coupon or done something fraudulent. We suggest cutting them out on the outside of the code around the edges and you will have fewer questions when using them. The outside code includes your IP address, which shows that the coupons are legitimate. All IPs are attached to your IP address, and it is not a good idea to trade them. You should never purchase or sell an Internet Printable coupon. If they fall into the wrong hands and are used fraudulently, then you will be held liable because they are linked to your IP address.

We always say that if a coupon sounds too good to be true, it probably is. A manufacturer is typically not going to provide a really high value coupon or a free product coupon in a large quantity. This holds true for a scanned coupon. If a person was given a high-end coupon, it should not be scanned, copied, or printed to be used for additional prints. You should avoid using a coupon that is in a PDF for a free product. Oftentimes it has been scanned or the expiration date or value could have been altered. If a coupon comes in a forwarded email and not from the original source, it is typically fraudulent, and we would not suggest using it. To find coupons that are fraudulent, visit Coupon Information Corporation, a non-profit that fights coupon fraud. Visit couponinformationcenter.com for more information.

"Bricks" Coupons are IPs. They are normally high-value coupons. You will know it is a "bricks" coupon because the URL will tell you. After you hit print, you will see a printer with three blinking dots sending to a picture of a printer. You can normally hit the backspace key three times after you see the blinking dots, and it will print a second copy for you. Bricks coupons are typically hot coupons and will not last long. They also have a print limit. When you find a bricks coupon, we suggest printing it, as they typically will run out of prints. If you want additional copies, you will need an additional computer to print from. If you have problems printing an IP coupon or can't install the printer, oftentimes there is a button to click. You can then submit your address and ask for the coupon to be mailed to you by simply filling out the form. This is a great way to still get the coupon when you have printer issues.

Some stores accept digital coupons that you load to your shopper's loyalty card or cell phone. Resources for digital coupons include Cellfire.com, Shortcuts.com, Kroger.com, Target.com, Meijer.com /Mperks, and PGeSaver.com. You can sign up and load your digital coupons at StockpilingMoms.com. These coupons typically do not double, if your store doubles coupons. Sometimes these coupons do stack, though! As we discussed, digital coupons can be a great way to get even more savings. Always check with your store's coupon policy to see if they accept digital coupons and if they stack with paper coupons.

An additional source for coupons is *All You* magazine. You can purchase *All You* only at Walmart or through a subscription. You can purchase a discounted subscription at StockpilingMoms.com. In just two months, we got our money back from our subscriptions via the coupons offered in the magazine. Each month, there are dozens of coupons in the magazine, including values up to $70 per month. We suggest purchasing subscriptions in quantities of two to take advantage of Buy One Get One Free sales. Also, you can visit AllYou.com for additional coupons and moneysaving offers online. The magazine is a fabulous resource of information, including recipes; menu planning; and money-saving ideas, tips, and articles.

We get many free coupons and special offers electronically, but in order to get those, you must sign up with a valid email. You don't want that to be an email that gets sent to your phone, in most cases. Our suggestion is to create an email address for couponing you don't use except for couponing or for junk purposes. This would be an address you don't have to check on a daily basis so that your regular email address doesn't collect spam. It will be for signing up for coupons, freebies, special offers, and joining e-clubs. You can use a simple password you will always remember such as "coupon" or "coupon1." The reason we suggest creating a junk email account is that you are going to need to sign up for a variety of accounts and offers to cash in on the great freebies that come along. By creating and using a junk email account, you will save yourself a lot of time and energy, and your inbox won't get filled up with offers and updates.

In addition, we suggest always protecting your identity. Most companies are looking for you to be of legal age (over eighteen) and that you have a valid email or mailing address. That being said, you should never give out your social security number or any information you feel uncomfortable with. In fact, if you were born on August 10, 1975, you could use 8/1/75 as your birth date when signing up for freebies because it is close to your birth date without giving out the exact date. We also suggest using your cell phone number, if necessary, as well. Never give any information that you don't feel comfortable giving.

Coupon Organization

After you have collected your coupons, what do you do next? It can be overwhelming when you start stockpiling, so coupon organization is a very important part to stockpiling success. If your coupons are unorganized, then you are simply not going to be able to save as much money. We suggest clipping all of your coupons. If you don't have your coupons clipped, then you won't be able to use them when you come across a great sale or clearance item in the store. We feel you are rewarded for clipping all coupons by being able to get in on the deals when you come across a great clearance deal, unadvertised special, or manager's special, so it is worth the time you invest in clipping each week.

We use the method of a binder filled with baseball card inserts. There are also pocket inserts that hold three or six coupons per page. We personally love the binder method because we can easily scan through and see very quickly what coupons we have available. By clipping and filing all of your coupons, you are able to match a coupon to an unadvertised or clearance deal when shopping in the stores. We personally

> **Tip:**
>
> If the coupon is at home, you're not getting the great deals at the store!

clip all the coupons that we will possibly ever use. The reason we clip all of our coupons is that although we may not buy a particular brand or item "normally," we would buy it if it were free or nearly free when matched with a coupon. Another stockpiling tip: if the coupon is at home filed or unclipped, then you are not able to get the deal at the store when you find it. Always clip and file your coupons and stay organized. We spend on average one hour a week clipping and organizing our coupons.

Melissa uses the Coupon Clutch (CouponClutch.com) to organize her coupons because it closes shut, she can carry it on her shoulder, and it is stylish. There is no reason why you can't be fashionable when using coupons! Shelley uses the Coupon Magic Organizer (CouponMagicOrganizer.com). We find these are the easiest ways to be able to carry our coupons, shop, and keep organized. We have dropped our binders several times in the checkout process, and having a binder that closes has become a huge lifesaver. The Coupon Clutch comes in a two- or three-inch version and in a variety of fabrics. You can even change the cover.

Another alternative to the Coupon Clutch is to use a binder with a shoulder strap that zips closed. There are a variety of choices, like the Coupon Magic Organizer (CouponMagicOrganizer.com), at most office supply stores. Regardless of what you choose, we suggest you invest in one when you start stockpiling. We also use two three-holed, zippered pouches at the front of our binder. One holds "hot coupons" that we don't want to file at the risk of not using them before expiration, and the other holds restaurant coupons. Also in our binder, we keep a calculator, a small pair of scissors, and the current weekly sales ads for price matching. It is very important to label your binder with your name and phone number in case it is lost or stolen. We suggest placing your cell phone number so that you can be contacted quickly.

We have our coupons divided into categories that make sense to us, and we suggest you do the same. We have them divided by: Baking, Beverages, Breakfast, Candy, Canned, Dairy, Frozen, Health and Beauty, Household, Fruits/Veggies, Meat, Organic, Other, Over-the-Counter Medicine, Rebates, Retail, and Store coupons. However it is important to create categories that make sense to you personally. You may choose to divide your categories even further, such as: Baby, Baking, Beverage, Bread, Breakfast, Candy, Canned, Cereal, Cleaning, Condiment, Dairy, Frozen, Health and Beauty, Laundry, Meat, Over-the-Counter Medicine, Paper, Pasta, Pet, Produce, Snacks, Rebates, Retail, and Store coupons.

Finding a system that makes sense to you will help with keeping the process smooth. Another idea is to organize your binder based on the aisles at your store. However, if you shop at a variety of stores, this may not work for you. We use plastic dividers with pockets between each section of our binder. We like having pockets to place large quantities of coupons or coupons nearing expiration. Another idea is to create a binder for household, health and beauty, and over-the-counter medicine, and another binder for general grocery items. We suggest keeping your binder organized and easy to carry. We don't suggest a binder that weighs ten pounds or more. You need to keep it simple and manageable. If you are juggling kids, keys, groceries, and your binder, it is easy to get overwhelmed. Start with a two-inch binder and increase the size if you need to. We also suggest not carrying a purse but considering instead attaching a wristlet to your binder and including your keys inside. We will go into safety concerns of why later in the book.

If you don't clip all the coupons from the inserts, it is important to keep and file the inserts (or what is left after you clip them). You can file them in a notebook using clear sheet protectors or place them on a shelf or in a hanging file folder. A stockpiling tip to know is that the date and name of the insert is printed in very fine print on the outside edge of each coupon insert cover. This helps later if you are searching for a coupon by insert date. We like to take a permanent marker and place the date on the front cover when it arrives. This helps to find coupons quickly if we are looking for them after they are filed. Keeping your leftover inserts neatly filed will save you time and money if you don't clip all of your coupons.

Being organized will take time in the beginning; however, once you are organized, it will end up saving you money in the end! We also want to add that we never leave home without our binders. We take them with us every time we leave the house. The one big tip we can give you is if you don't have all of your coupons with you, then you won't be able to save money when you run across a great deal! We don't suggest pulling your coupons that you plan to use before a shopping trip. Instead, we suggest pulling them when you place the item into your cart. If you pull them in advance, you have the chance they could be lost, and if an item is not in stock, then you are faced with having to re-file, which takes additional time and energy. It is simply a better strategy to pull the coupon after the item is in the cart, again saving you time and money. We suggest purchasing a third zipper pouch or carrying an envelope to place your pulled coupon into once you have placed the item into your cart.

We also want to share with you our technique for organizing our clipped coupons. We clip our coupons on Sunday evening with scissors, a paper cutter, or a razor blade. If we are doing more than one of the same insert at a time, then we use a razor blade or paper cutter to make the process quicker. Simply take apart your inserts, stack them by pages, and staple the coupons together so that they don't move when you cut them. By using a razor blade or paper cutter, you are able to quickly cut out multiple copies of the same coupon, and because they are stapled together, they can be stacked and later filed. This is a huge time saver. You do have to be careful not to do too many inserts at the same time so they don't move on you. Also remember that you need the complete expiration date and UPC code in order to redeem your coupons.

On Monday morning, we file our coupons. We normally purchase four to ten inserts each week, and we collect inserts from our friends. We also target hot coupons and order larger quantities from coupon clipping services. If you use a coupon clipper, then place an order over the weekend and then file the coupons when they arrive in the mail. We supplement by ordering clipped coupons, especially on items that we want to stockpile! Not only is it a great way to get multiple copies of the coupon, but it also helps save the environment because you are not purchasing multiple papers.

After we clip our coupons, we file them into our binder by section. It is important to keep your coupons clipped, filed, and organized so that you are ready for shopping trips. If you keep up on filing your coupons weekly, you will not become overwhelmed and will always be able to get in on all the great deals and clearance finds. There is nothing worse than drowning in a sea of coupon inserts.

It is very important to use coupons correctly. Coupons should be used based on the wording on the coupon not what is pictured. If you are trying to use a coupon for a product other than what is worded on the coupon, that is coupon fraud. The store will not be reimbursed for that item, and it is not legal. It not only hurts honest couponers, but it also hurts the store. If a coupon says $1/2, then you must purchase two items. If it says $1 off one 32-oz. bottle, then you must purchase a 32–oz. bottle. It is very important that you do not use a coupon on a product that is not included in the wording even if that product is in the same brand family. For example, if the coupon says $1 off any whole wheat pasta, the coupon should not be used on white pasta but only on whole wheat pasta even if the coupon scans properly and does not beep. If the coupon says $1 off any pasta, then it can be used on any variety of pasta. It is not legitimate to try to match coding from a coupon to a product. The coupon should only be used based on the wording on the coupon.

However, remember that if the coupon says "off any one," then you may use that coupon on any product size. It should also only be used with a current expiration date, unless your store accepts expired coupons (which most don't). Using expired coupons without permission is not legal. It not only hurts honest couponers, but it also hurts the store. The store will not get reimbursed when you use an expired coupon. Just because an expired coupon is accepted or does not beep does not mean that it is OK to use it.

We often get asked what it means when a coupon says "one per purchase." This simply means that you can only use one coupon per item purchased. Each item is a purchase, so you can purchase multiple items and use multiple coupons, unless the coupon reads $2 on 2, which means you would have to purchase two items to use the one coupon. So for example, if you want to use multiple coupons, then you have to purchase multiple items. Make sense? Now let's take it one step further. What if it says "one per transaction"? This means you can use only one coupon for the purchase. All combined items paid for at the same time equate a transaction. Then you would need to make multiple transactions in order to use additional coupons. You could do that in a variety of ways. You can simply put the bar down and break your order into multiple transactions on the conveyer belt. Tell the cashier that you are going to make multiple transactions and pay for each one individually, using a coupon for each transaction.

If you don't feel comfortable making multiple transactions, another choice is to go through the checkout process multiple times and make several transactions. You can take your purchase to your car and walk back in and make another purchase. We normally limit ourselves to two transactions per checkout so as to not hold the line up, unless the store is not crowded and the cashier is willing.

However, if the coupon reads "Limit 1 transaction per day," you are going to need to bring an additional person with you to make multiple transactions. This can include your children. Our sons have been using coupons since they were three years old so that we could make more than one transaction per day. This is a great way to get them involved and for you to be able to make multiple transactions. Another option is to bring your spouse or friends and ask them to make a transaction for you or to come back daily for additional transactions.

When a coupon says "one per visit," you can use only one coupon per visit; however, typically leaving the store and coming back in counts as a visit. The same process as above would apply. When it says one per customer, you will need to take a family member along with you. Each of you is considered a customer. We often take our sons with us, and they count! If we want more items, then we take our husbands or other family members and friends too! If it says one per household, you are limited to one per household, or mailing address, and that is it. This often refers to rebates or limits to a store loyalty or shopper's card.

When a coupon states "get this free when you buy that" (WYB), you can use one coupon for the "that" and the WYB will be for the "this" item. So for example, if you have a coupon that says get this body wash free when you buy that deodorant, you can use a coupon for the deodorant and get the body wash free using the "when you buy that" coupon. This is another way to save! The dollar coupon applies toward your out of pocket expense for the item you purchased, bringing your savings higher.

Many stores offer 10 for 10 specials. These are great sales! You do not have to purchase ten of the same item or even ten items total to qualify for the $1 per item pricing. You can purchase one item or as many as you want. This is normally true for 2/$5 or 2/$4 sales too. This is another helpful stockpiling tip to know.

Buy One Get One Free (BOGO) coupons mean that with one coupon you are buying one product and getting one free. At many stores, you can use a coupon on the free product! This brings your out-of-pocket expense lower by using a coupon on the free product. So for example, a Buy One Get One Free deodorant coupon could be matched with one $2 off deodorant coupon, and the $2 off would apply toward the product you are purchasing because you are already getting one item for free. This is a great way to save!

At most stores you can also stack a Buy One Get One Free offer from the store with a Buy One Get One Free manufacturer coupon. When you match the two, you can get both items for free. The manufacturer pays for one, and the store pays for the other, again depending on your store's coupon policy. Most stores will allow you to use a dollar-off coupon too, making this a moneymaker. Strategically using BOGO coupons and store offers is a great way to bump up your savings.

As a rule of etiquette, please don't clear shelves. Many people ask us how we stockpile so much and leave something for someone else. Well, there is a way and we stockpile by these rules. Do not buy more than ten like items in any given shopping trip. We never buy more than ten similar items at a time no matter how many coupons we have. The only exception is a 10 for $10, get the 11th item for free sale. Consider shopping at multiple locations. We do this often. We have multiple stores located within ten miles of each other. When we know we will be near a store, we will stop and make a purchase. There are times we will go to the farthest store in our area because on the way home we pass the other three. We will buy our frozen and refrigerated items at the last stop. This way we can get up to forty of the item we want at different stores and never clear a shelf in the process.

If we have more coupons to use, we will go the last day of the sale and buy more. If the store is out, we will ask for a rain check and buy the ten items another time. Always have a plan when you are stockpiling. If you are shopping a sale where you have to buy a certain number of qualifying items to get a discount (like a Mega sale at Kroger), you have to plan ahead. Be prepared to substitute another item for one if they are out of inventory or plan to get a rain check and come back another date. We plan a list of filler items that are already matched with coupons. If we do not have any more coupons, we look for the item that has the absolute lowest price. When you get to the store and they are out of the items you want, it can be very frustrating and can easily throw off your plan, so it is best to be prepared.

Another option is to place an order with your store if you want to order a large number of items. Simply ask to speak with a manager or place an order at the customer service desk. There are times you may want to stockpile a large quantity of an item and placing an order is the best way to go. If you want a large quantity, you should order that item versus clearing shelves. Always remember there are people out there seeking the same deals as you. This is a great way to remove the frustrations from shopping, and you can use coupons when you place an order with no problem.

Shelley once saw an example of someone who was trying to clear a shelf. She was at a store with her family when a gentleman tried to purchase three grocery carts full of soft drinks. When someone tries to purchase such a large quantity, it makes it hard for other people to purchase the deal. The management got involved and told the gentleman he could not purchase all the soft drinks. Remember when stockpiling, the store usually has the right to limit, at their discretion. The gentleman ended up purchasing thirty soft drinks and leaving the rest for other shoppers. Be prepared that a manager may limit how many coupons you can use or items you can purchase if you are trying to clear a shelf. There is nothing more frustrating than a shelf clearer.

3

shopping strategies

After you have spent your time clipping, organizing, matching, and shopping, be sure that all your hard work pays off. Our suggestion is to always have an idea of what you think your total will be before checking out. Prior to checking out, we always count how many coupons we are using so that we know if they were all scanned. It is extremely important to pay attention during your checkout. We watch as each item is scanned to be sure that it rings with the correct price and as every coupon is scanned to see that it is removed from our total (and doubles, if applicable).

What we have found (the hard way) is that if you are not very aware during checkout, then all of your hard work may be for nothing. Often a cashier can look like he's using all the coupons when he might not be. We have found that particularly when you are using a large number of coupons, they might stick together or a cashier may skip some. Also, if a coupon beeps, then the cashier will have to manually enter or override it, and often they don't (even if it looks like they are). Watch the total and be sure each coupon comes off of your total when you check out.

As a final check, we count the total number of coupons on our receipt before we leave the store to see if it matches the number of coupons that we used. If not, then we immediately go to the customer service desk to get the cash for the missing coupon. After we get home, we enter our savings into an excel spreadsheet and file every receipt so that if we find a rebate, we are able to submit it for additional savings.

Product	Company	Submitted	Received	Amount

It is easy to get distracted when shopping with a child or when someone strikes up a conversation during your checkout. Melissa had an experience where a customer checking out behind her started a conversation and she was not able to pay attention to the cashier. As a result, she ended up not saving $18 from the sale. This made a huge difference in her savings. She ended up taking her items and receipt back and got $14 in cash back because some of the store coupons scanned as "0," so she had proof. As for the $4 in manufacturer coupons, there was no way to prove that they had been used, so she lost that $4 in savings. She learned the hard way to pay attention during checkout and not to let others distract her.

Another key to stockpiling success is strategic cashier selection. We always talk about strategic coupon use; we think that just as important is strategic cashier selection. We are going to be honest that our target cashier is the high school–aged, male cashier. Why? Normally we get the best service and least hassle. One, he doesn't complain about how many coupons we use. Two, he doesn't mind if a coupon beeps and he manually enters it. Three, he loves to see how much we save. Four, he smiles and enjoys the checkout process with us. And five, he doesn't mind if we break our order into multiple transactions.

If there is not a high school–aged, male cashier, then our second choice is a high school–aged, female cashier. They are usually just as friendly but maybe don't enjoy the checkout process with us as much as the male does. It's generally still a very positive checkout experience for us. Who we do not like to check out with is the fifty- to sixty-year-old female cashier. We typically avoid that cashier's lane at all costs, even if that means we will have to wait in line for another cashier.

In addition, we do not like to check out with the fifty- to sixty-year-old male cashier. Normally these cashiers are not as friendly, and we find they tell us a coupon is not valid before even trying to scan it. They gruff and grumble under their breath, oftentimes saying that we are "stealing" from the store. In general, they are not a pleasure to check out with, and therefore we personally make the decision to avoid them (even if that means we wait longer to check out). We are not trying to offend, but based on our shopping experience, this is the reality. *Please do not take offense if you are a cashier ages fifty to sixty. This is just our opinion as consumers.*

In addition, we choose not to use a self-checkout lane. When using coupons, in particular for a large order, we find that it takes on average three times as long to check out at the self-checkout because the coupons will have to be manually accepted by the self-checkout cashier. We have tried it on several occasions, and to us, it is not worth the time or effort. This does not hold true if you are only purchasing one or two items; however, in general they are not our favorite method of checking out.

We also do not use the express checkout lane when we are using coupons as a courtesy to other shoppers. Because of the time it takes to check out, we find that the express lane cashier is in a huge rush to get us in and out and therefore doesn't take the time necessary to make sure all the coupons scan appropriately. So in general, the express lane is one we avoid, and we find fewer cashier errors as a result.

Shopping with Your Kids

We always recommend that, if possible, you avoid couponing with your children; however, that is not always possible. In fact, for many of us, shopping with our children is our only option. We built our stockpiles with our children in tow, and we want to share with you some strategies to make the experience positive for both you and your children.

We always look for inexpensive ways to reward our children as we shop. It is amazing to us what entertains them and what simple steps we can do to include them in the process. By including your children in the process, not only will the experience be more pleasant, you will also teach them how to be frugal. Encourage your children to look for coupons for you when shopping. Melissa's son has his own coupon binder (which is simply a half-inch binder) that he places his coupons in that he collects at the store.

Encouraging your children to be part of the process not only teaches them to value money but also instills in them that coupons are a great way to save money. Our children know that we don't buy anything without a coupon. There is no asking for items in the store because they know the answer is no. We stick to our list and don't place items in our cart that are not on sale matched with a coupon. This really helps avoid meltdowns at the store because going into the store, our children know it is not OK to ask for items that are not on the list.

Make a shopping list for your child. We make a special list for our children to carry at the store. They always want to hold our list, so if they have their own, it works out better for us. We include a few of their favorite items on the list and give them a crayon to mark off the items as we put them in the cart. This keeps them engaged as we shop, and they are busy looking for their items to place in the cart versus finding items that are not on sale to put in the cart.

Pack a snack from home for your child. It is easy to get hungry at the store when you see food, so instead of opening up a package or purchasing something just to avoid a meltdown, plan ahead and pack a snack from home. This will save you in the long run. When we shop at stores that have small, child-size carts, we allow our children to push them. They can sometimes be daredevils with the carts, so this is only allowed if they can control themselves and if it is not at a busy time of the day. Another idea is to bring a book or other activity for your child to do while shopping.

Find inexpensive or free rewards for your children. Our children love to see the lobsters at the grocery stores. We strategically plan our list to end by the lobsters and use this as an incentive to get our shopping done without meltdowns. This is a free incentive that works well for our children. Sometimes we are really lucky and the meat department will get them out for the children to see up close. Another reward for our children is visiting the fish aquariums. If the store where we are shopping has live fish aquariums, this is another built-in incentive for them. What is great is to find out what time your store feeds because the fish are very active. Oftentimes the store will even allow our children to participate in feeding the fish, which is a huge treat!

Use your shopping trip as a learning experience. We take time to show our children a variety of foods in the store as an opportunity to teach them about new foods. We like to show them fruits and vegetables that they may have seen on a kids' program and extend their learning into real life. Or we talk about how we could plant that food in our garden. It is a great opportunity to teach while you shop. We also allow them to taste new foods when the store has samples available.

Pack a special treat from home for checkout. To avoid spending in the check out aisle, we pack a small treat or reward from home. This could be a sucker, a small box of candy, or fruit snacks. As we are heading to the checkout, we pull out the treat so that we have the precious few minutes we need while checking out. If you don't keep score at checkout, you will possibly not do as well as you hoped, so these five minutes of uninterrupted time are so valuable! Packing a treat from home is a key to your success! Melissa often says that her son's hair could be on fire, but for those five minutes, she will not be interrupted.

We also love our store's $0.01 pony rides. After we check out, we are sure to let our kids ride the pony for a penny! Even if your store doesn't offer a penny pony ride, a $0.25 ride is still a great deal and possible incentive for your child. If we are shopping at Target, we allow our children to buy a popcorn or drink from the Target Cafe. It is the best $1.50 we spend while shopping! We swing in and pick it up, and they eat for the entire trip. In fact, our children often ask when we can go to Target to use coupons (and of course, to get popcorn).

We hope some of these ideas help you while you are shopping with your children. If you try to make your experience fun for all of you, we promise that in the end you will enjoy shopping with your children. If you teach your children at a young age about coupon use and the techniques of stockpiling, you will raise frugal children. Our children already know about coupons, rock bottom pricing, and stockpiling. This is because they are a part of the process.

Safety First

We want to be sure to discuss safety when it comes to stockpiling. Not too long ago, a friend of Shelley's was approached in a grocery store parking lot. They stole her car and purse, but she was left unharmed. This really made us think of the safety issues associated with shopping. The reason shoppers are often victims is that they have money, credit cards, and children and often are preoccupied with their purchases and getting everything in the car. We know as a stockpiler we are often really excited about our purchases and our "coupon high" and how much we did not spend! As we think more about our exit from the store, we are probably not as aware as we should be. So here are some ideas for safe shopping.

If you are shopping after dark, shop with an adult family member or friend. Carry a very small amount of cash or just the credit card you are using for that particular shopping trip with your driver's license. We actually put our credit card, license, and some cash in our coupon binder so we do not have to carry a purse. If possible, leave small children at home. We know some people do not have this option. If you shop with your children, never leave them unattended or out of your sight. After exiting the store, we always put our children in the car first, lock the car doors, and then put our groceries in. At night, we often get in the car, lock the doors, and then turn to buckle the children in. There is nothing more frightening than the thought of someone taking our boys.

If you carry a purse into the store, do not leave your purse unattended in the cart. It only takes a second for someone to steal your purse. Always put your credit card or cash away before walking out of the store. You should never leave the store with cash in hand. Also don't leave the store distracted. Check your receipt before you leave the store. If you have math errors on your receipt, look before leaving the store, not on your way to the car. Always pull your keys out before you exit the store. Always park your car in a visible and well-lit section of the parking lot. Try not to forget where you park. We always try to park in the same area and, at night, as close to a lamp post or cart corral as possible. Don't forget you have a horn in your car. If someone approaches you while you are in your car, blow it or use your horn feature on your key fob if you have one. Always keep your cell phone in your pocket in case you need to use it. Avoid talking on the phone as you walk to your car because it will distract you from being aware of your surroundings. Keeping yourself safe is more important than coupons or how much you saved. Celebrate once you are in the car.

Dealing with Criticism

How should you deal with stockpiling criticism? This is a very important topic in our couponing and stockpiling world. We often face a lot of criticism from people behind us in line, cashiers, and people who hear us say the word "stockpile." When someone sees you purchasing multiple quantities of an item, they may make a rude comment to you. Typically they are really just interested in why you are purchasing that amount of a single item. When we receive stockpiling criticism, we just tell them the facts. First and foremost, we only stockpile for our families and to donate. You can say, "This is for our family. This is how we are able to stay home with our children and provide for them."

The criticism we receive from other shoppers in the store is aggravating, but sometimes we make it a laughing matter. If you receive a comment from a rude shopper behind you in line, you can choose to ignore them or you can always say something like "Don't be jealous that I am only paying an eighth of what you are paying for fewer items." We are happy to put a shopper in his place if he is rude to us. We have the same rights as others to check out without harassment.

Criticism from cashiers is easy to take care of. If a cashier is rude to you or makes rude comments, we suggest being polite and then asking to speak to a customer service manager or the store manager. It is not beneficial to argue with a cashier. You can always walk away from your order to the customer service desk and ask for help with the situation. Remember, stockpiling is legal. As long as you are not committing coupon fraud, there is no reason for you to have any mistreatment at the store. Stockpiling is smart. Stockpiling leaves extra money for your family. Stockpiling allows you to have fewer trips to the grocery store. Stockpiling allows you to have on hand what your family likes. Stockpiling is a way of life. There is no reason for you to have to endure any form of criticism when you shop, and by taking a stand, you will not have to.

In some cases, for example, if you have a bad experience or you find that the store will not uphold the store coupon policy, you will find it necessary to file a complaint with the store's corporate head-quarters. If you are able to get a corporate coupon policy from a store, we suggest carrying a copy in your coupon binder. This will often end issues when you are trying to use a coupon. However, if it doesn't end the situation, never pay for an item that you feel you should not pay for. Walk away from the transaction. Ask for your coupons back and leave the store. Always document the cashier name or any other staff names so that when you file your complaint with corporate, you have the information necessary to remedy the situation. We actually carry the corporate numbers with us at all times when we are shopping.

Shopping Online

Another shopping strategy is to shop online. One great resource is Amazon.com. We post Amazon.com deals at StockpilingMoms .com. You can purchase some grocery items online, getting a great deal on organic, gluten free, and some household and personal care items in particular. Another benefit to using Amazon.com is that you can redeem your Swag Bucks for Amazon.com gift cards (which we will discuss more in chapter 11). This brings your out-of-pocket expense even lower! You can also sign up for the Amazon app, which can help you get in on deals before they expire. It is a great resource.

There are several benefits to shopping online. One is that it takes very little time, and there is no travel cost involved. Oftentimes you can get free shipping offers. If you are going to shop through

Amazon.com, we suggest checking out Amazon Mom. It is a great resource for diapers in particular. Go to: https://www.amazon .com/gp/mom/signup/welcome and sign up. Simply search for your favorite brand of diapers. Then select subscribe and save, determine how often you want shipments sent to you, and enjoy the rewards. What is nice is that you can change your subscription at any time. They also offer free two-day shipping. You get a free enrollment to Amazon Prime when you purchase $25 or more in diapers per week (they use the retail cost of your diapers to determine this rather than your discounted total). You also have the ability to change or cancel your subscription at any time. Shopping online can be a great alternative, and often you can find some great deals. If you are using diapers, we suggest checking out Amazon Mom.

4

storage

It is very important to organize your stockpile. This has been a growth process for us. As our stockpile has grown, we have had to change the location or add to it. We started in our pantries, which we quickly outgrew. Next, we put our stockpiles in our basements, and they quickly became unorganized and messy. At that point, we decided it was time to build stockpile shelving in our unfinished basement. We suggest that if you have a basement, you locate your stockpile there. It is worth clearing some clutter for your stockpile.

We do not suggest that you store your items in your garage because you have to factor in that the temperature does not remain constant, causing problems such as your stockpile freezing or melting. This will affect many items and can potentially ruin them. Also, animals and bugs could compromise your stockpile. Store foods in cool cabinets and away from appliances that produce heat. Make sure your storage is away from water heaters, furnaces, and so on. It is also best to choose a cool, dry place that is off of the ground for most items you stockpile.

How do you stockpile with little storage? We always say to people who take our classes, if there is a will, there is a way! Think outside of the box when it comes to storing your stockpile. Never let the excuse "I don't have the room to stockpile" stop you from saving thousands of dollars a year. Just remove the clutter and find your stockpile a new home! You may have to get creative when it comes to storing your stockpile, but not having room is not an excuse. If you do not have shelving you can spare in your basement or don't have a basement, you could consider buying a storage cabinet, which you could place in a guest bedroom or in the corner of your dining room, office, or kitchen.

Utilize your kitchen. Store your stockpile in your pantry and cabinets. Remove items that you are not using that take up a lot of space and utilize the space that you have. Get a shoe organizer and hang it on the inside of your pantry door. Consider storing kitchen items that you are no longer using under beds or place them in your garage or basement. Melissa removed a wok from her kitchen, and Shelley purged tons of kitchen appliances she was not using to make room for her stockpile.

You could also store your stockpile in your linen closet. In our opinion, sheets, blankets, and pillows are taking up valuable real estate. Store your stockpile in your linen closet and store linens under the bed. You could even use space saver bags! Shelley repurposed her linen closet to store health and beauty aids and other items. Purchase a storage cabinet. Though it may not be appealing to have a storage cabinet in your dining room, what is more important, saving money and having the space to store your stockpile, or having a perfect home but being unable to stockpile? We choose the stockpile every time! Melissa has a storage cabinet in the corner of her office where she stores her health and beauty aids. It may not be attractive, but it gets the job done.

Consider using your children's closets. Use the top rack to store items for your stockpile. Most children do not have a full closet, so this allows you to use the extra room. If you have an extra bedroom, utilize it for stockpile storage. Use your guest bedroom's closet for your stockpile, or better yet, turn it into your stockpile room. Consider under-the-bed storage. This is an area that most of us don't think about. Melissa bought risers when she lived in a bi-level and they were running out of storage space and used under-the-bed storage boxes for items that she didn't use often. This is also the perfect location for personal hygiene, cereal, paper goods, and canned goods!

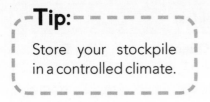

Tip:

Store your stockpile in a controlled climate.

Use bathroom storage. Utilize the space under your bathroom sink for stockpiling storage. You can fit so much into this area (trust us, we know). You can even purchase shelving or use baskets under your sink for the stacking of stockpile items. Consider a shoe organizer for behind the door to store what you use on a daily basis and use the space under the sink for your stockpile. If you are creative, you will find a location for your stockpile. Keep in mind that you need room for your stockpile to grow, you need space so that you can see what you have, and you need to be able to access your stockpile. We like being able to stand in front of our stockpiles when we "shop" from them. Our number one stockpile storage tip to remember is to store your stockpile in a controlled climate.

We personally organize our stockpile by categories, similar to how we organize our coupon binder. In our opinion, organizing your stockpile is as important as building it. If you don't keep it organized, you don't know what you have and you can't use it effectively. If you continue to purchase items that you don't need, then you are not saving money but wasting it.

It is also important to inventory your stockpile. When we first started stockpiling, we thought we had a fairly good idea of what was in it. We did for the first several months, but after that we would come home from shopping and realize that we already had more than enough of an item in our current stockpile or items of similar expiration date. That was when we decided it was time to inventory our stockpile.

We use an excel spreadsheet to inventory our stockpile. It is categorized in the same manner as our coupon binder. Under each category, we include the name, amount, and expiration date of every single item in our stockpile. This is a great way to know what you have at any given time, and it keeps you from overpurchasing or running out of an item. The following is a sample of our inventory spreadsheet:

Breakfast		
Item Description	Quantity	Exp. Date

In terms of expiration dates, it is important that you use your stockpile before it expires. If not, you have wasted your time, energy, and money that you have invested into building it. We recommend that you use FIFO (First In, First Out). This is a method used by grocery stores and in the food service industry. When we began stockpiling, we started using FIFO in order to maintain freshness and to be certain that we did not waste our money. It is easy to do. When you replace stock, make sure the items with the closest expiration dates remain at the front. Stock your new inventory in the back, and that way it rotates and is used before it expires.

A trick that Shelley learned in her days as a server is to label, date, and rotate. If an item does not have an expiration date, then we mark it with the purchase date with a permanent marker. Make sure to date foods when you buy them and rotate accordingly. Always use the oldest first. Foods stored for longer than recommended or beyond the date on the package may change quality, color, and flavor. Where you live may also affect the recommended storage time. Warm and humid conditions shorten the shelf life of goods, and how you store your stockpile will affect the quality.

Expiration Dates

When you are grocery shopping, check the expiration dates. It is not a great deal if you purchase multiples of expired or near expiration foods. We always double-check every item's expiration date before putting it into our cart to be sure we are really getting a great deal. This is important for canned goods and cereal in particular. Also, buy new-looking or fresh packages. Dusty cans indicate old stock. Do not purchase dented or bulging cans because you risk contaminating your family. Don't be tempted to buy the old stock unless you plan to use it right away. This is not an item to stockpile.

Manufacturers use what is called "open dating." In open dating, a manufacturer uses a calendar date to help store managers determine how long they should keep the food items for sale. There are four types of open dating: sell by or pull dates, best if used by dates, expiration dates, and pack dates. It is important to understand open dating terms so that you can get the most out of your stockpile. We will explain each type.

Sell by dates or pull dates are pretty self-explanatory. This is a date the item should be sold by. These items are usually still good after the date, but the manufacturer wants the product pulled after that date. It is kind of like smelling the milk after the sell by date or expiration date: use good judgment. Most stores will not sell an item after the open dating has passed.

Best if used by dates are much like sell by dates. This date means the product will be at its highest quality and will taste best before this time. As long as the product is properly stored and there are no signs of spoilage, the product is safe to use. Again, smell the milk. If it doesn't smell or look safe, then you should not consume it.

An expiration date is the last date the food should be consumed. The only exception is eggs. Eggs are normally good for thirty days from expiration. However, you should not buy eggs that are already expired. As they age, the quality will decrease.

The pack date is the date the product was packaged. This gives you an idea of how fresh a product is by knowing what date it was packaged for sale.

We frequently check the expiration dates of our stockpiles on our excel spreadsheets. That way if we notice something is nearing expiration, then we are able to include this ingredient in our menu planning or donate the product. In our opinion, menu planning and frugal living go hand in hand. We will further discuss both later in the book.

Freezing Foods

When we started stockpiling, neither of us had a deep freezer. Shelley got one first, and Melissa had "freezer envy." Melissa was thrilled when she got one for Christmas 2009! It was one of the best gifts she ever got. If you are going to stockpile, we highly suggest investing in a deep freezer. It is the best investment for your return. We are often asked about how to select a deep freezer or if we know of any good freezer sales. We both have an upright deep freezer, and our best advice to you is to factor in the following before you make a purchase.

The first thing to decide is whether you want a chest or an upright freezer. We have used both kinds and by far prefer the upright. The ease of being able to open the door and quickly see what we have is what made our decision. However, if you look at the cost of each, you may find that a chest freezer is in your price range. And if you inventory your stockpile and stay organized, that will help you know what's there if you choose a chest freezer. Keep a detailed inventory and check off items after they are used. You can slip it into a plastic sheet protector and attach it to the freezer door.

Next consider size. In our opinion, bigger is better. We both chose a 27-cubic-foot freezer and can remember thinking how big it was and wondering how we would ever fill it. Now we look back at that and laugh. If we were purchasing again, we would definitely go bigger. If you are considering purchasing a side of beef or freezing milk, loaves of bread, or cartons of juice, it will fill your freezer in no time. Many stockpilers have more than one freezer.

A major consideration for us was energy efficiency. We wanted a deep freezer that would be energy efficient. This is something that you may want to consider when making a purchase. The freezer will highlight if it is an Energy Star appliance or not.

Finally, something else to consider is if your deep freezer should have a lock on it. This is something that we personally wanted for safety and control.

When it comes to making a purchase, our best tip is to compare prices. Look at the stores that you have available to you and shop around. Also, consider any incentives that your store has for you to shop there, like a rewards program or other available discounts. We find that September and October seem to be the best times of year as far as sales for major appliances because manufacturers are releasing their new models for the upcoming year and stores want to deplete their current inventory. Another idea is to look for floor samples or scratch and dent appliances for a deeper discount.

In addition to our kitchen refrigerators, we also each have a second refrigerator for additional stockpiling. We suggest purchasing an inexpensive second refrigerator. Often you can get one from a friend who may be moving or through www.freecycle.org or www .craigslist.com. The investment is worthwhile because you are adding additional space to be able to stockpile. The second appliance could be placed in your basement or garage; just be sure it is properly installed.

Another key investment is the FoodSaver. The FoodSaver extends the life of your food and keeps it without freezer burn. We suggest buying it at Kohl's when you get a 30 percent off discount plus earn Kohl's Cash. There are often rebates too! You can also often find them for a great price at yard sales or Goodwill. The bags are expensive to use with it, but we feel it is very much worth the investment. You can purchase the bags at Kohl's when they're on sale, with a 30 percent off coupon plus earn Kohl's Cash. There are also generic brand bags that work with the FoodSaver.

There are a few tips that we want to share with you about using the FoodSaver. When you are freezing an item, it is best to "flash freeze" it, meaning that you want to lay it flat and freeze it until it is firm (two to three hours). After two to three hours, simply place the pre-frozen food into the food saver bags and seal them. Another stockpiling tip is that if you want the food to be moist after it's been frozen, then you'll want to use the moist setting. So for all meat, you would use the moist setting.

We love that you can thaw the meat directly from the freezer in the sealed package! It is also simple to mark directly onto the package with a permanent marker the date it was sealed. You can use the FoodSaver to extend the life of so many foods that you stockpile. In fact, the FoodSaver says that it extends the life of frozen items for up to two years! We use it for fruits, meat, poultry, fish, vegetables, and more! By using the FoodSaver, you can really extend the shelf life of foods.

When it comes to freezing your stockpile, you need to think outside of the box. In fact, there is actually very little you can't freeze. We freeze bread, buns, cheese, cream cheese, milk, orange juice, eggs, butter, meat, fruit, and vegetables to name a few. It is a great way to extend the life of your food. When you find a great deal, you can purchase a larger quantity when you freeze it.

Did you know that eggs can be frozen for up to one year? You don't freeze eggs in the shell; instead, remove them from the shells and mix them well (scramble) before freezing. After scrambling them, pour them into an ice cube tray and cover with saran wrap. They can be placed in a freezer-safe container after frozen or left in the tray until used. One large egg equals two ice cubes. Another idea is to freeze eggs in a freezer-safe storage bag. Lay them flat to freeze them to take up less room. Write the date on the freezer-safe container. For best results, eggs should be thawed in the refrigerator the day before you plan to use them.

Milk can be frozen; however, it may separate when thawed. Frozen milk is excellent for cooking and can be used for drinking but may need to be shaken between uses. Freeze milk by the gallon by removing some of the milk (1½ cups per gallon) so when the jug expands it doesn't overflow. You do not have to remove milk from a half gallon paper carton. Milk can be frozen for one month. Date the milk when freezing it. For best results, thaw it in the refrigerator, which takes several days, and shake it well before using. After thawing, the milk lasts for about a week. If you can pick up milk on a manager's special, this is a great way to save money from your family's budget.

Did you know you can freeze cottage cheese? The answer is yes and no. We know that sounds funny, but yes, you can freeze it. Will it be as good as if it had never been frozen? No. But it depends on how you plan to use it. You can freeze it directly in the original container or another airtight container. We have frozen it to be used in lasagna or other recipes with no problems. Depending on the size of curd, it may break down after thawed. We have found that fat-free and low-fat cottage cheeses do not freeze as well. We would suggest large curd, 2 percent or whole fat for best results. By freezing it, you can extend the life by four to six months. Just write the date you put it into the freezer with a permanent marker so you know how long it has been there. Ricotta cheese would be similar to the above. Again, when you find cottage cheese on a manager's special, it is a great time to pick up several and freeze them.

You can also freeze cream cheese. Will it be as good as if it had never been frozen? Again, that depends on how you plan to use it. You can freeze it directly in the original package. Freezing does change the consistency, but if you are using it in cooking, there is no concern. We use it for dips or other recipes that call for it. It can also be used for spreading, but we find it to be crumbly, so you have to use a spoon to smooth it back to a somewhat normal consistency. By freezing, you can extend the life of cream cheese by four to six months. Just write the date you put it into the freezer with a permanent marker so you know how long it has been frozen. You can often get cream cheese for free using a coupon, so this is a great item to stockpile.

Can you freeze cheese? The answer is yes! Cheese is easily frozen in the package from the store. Just date it with a permanent marker with the date you are freezing it and place it in the freezer. We find that shredded and block cheese freeze very well. We freeze cheese sticks and sliced cheese too! They can sometimes change consistency and become crumbled, but they are perfect for cooking with. By freezing, you extend the life of the cheese by four to six months past expiration or from the time you freeze them. You can also freeze cheese that is out of the original wrapper by placing it in plastic wrap and then into a freezer bag. We prefer the original package when possible. When thawing it, simply place it in your refrigerator until thawed and use it soon after. Remember to date it with a permanent marker before freezing it. Again, cheese is often free or near free and is a great stockpile item.

You can also freeze sour cream. However, again, it really depends on how you plan to use it. We do not freeze it on a regular basis, but it can be done. By freezing it, you can extend the life by four to six months. Just write the date you put it into the freezer with a permanent marker so you know how long it has been there. You can freeze it in the original container or another airtight container; however, freezing will affect the texture. It will turn it into the consistency of cottage cheese. So if you are going to use it for baking, then it would be OK, but if you are using it in its original form, then we would not recommend it. Also, another helpful tip is that you can extend the life of your sour cream by storing the unopened container upside down in your fridge. Several readers have told us this tip, and it works!

Recently, we had a great coupon that netted free hummus at our local grocery store. One of our readers, Jayme, emailed and asked if you could freeze hummus. She decided to give it a try since it was free and she had nothing to lose. The answer is, yes you can freeze hummus; however, depending on the manufacturer, it may alter its smooth and creamy texture after it has been frozen. If you freeze hummus, store it in an airtight, lidded plastic container. Leave about an inch of space to allow for the expansion that occurs when moist products freeze. Frozen hummus should be defrosted and consumed within five to seven days. Melissa has heard that adding a tablespoon of olive oil prior to freezing will help with the consistency. Our reader confirmed that the consistency changed after it was thawed, but it was edible. So the answer is yes, you can freeze hummus. We hope this helps those of you who love hummus like we do.

Another great item to freeze is bananas. If you have ever purchased too many bananas and been unable to eat them before they get too ripe or have found ripe bananas for a great price, a great alternative is to freeze them. You can freeze them and eat them by themselves for a special frozen treat or dip them in chocolate and roll them in nuts and then freeze them! We like to use frozen bananas in fruit smoothies because they make the smoothies have a cold and smooth texture.

There are several ways to freeze a banana, but our preferred method is to peel the banana, cut it into slices, and put the slices in freezer bags or freezer-safe containers. You can also freeze the banana whole in the peel. This is not our favorite method because we normally use frozen bananas for fruit smoothies, banana bread, or banana pudding. So having them sliced is better. Also, sometimes unpeeling a frozen banana can leave you with a mushy banana. When you freeze a banana in the peel, the peel will turn brown, but the fruit inside will be fine. For best results, if you plan to eat your banana, freeze it before it is overripe. If you are going to use it for a smoothie or for banana bread, you can freeze it even after the banana is overripe. It is a great way to stretch your dollar!

As you stockpile, keep in mind that you can freeze many items to extend their shelf lives and stretch your family's budget.

5

monthly menu planning

We suggest that if you stockpile, you should also use a monthly menu plan. We suggest creating one or two menus for spring and summer and one or two for fall and winter. If you use a monthly menu plan, you will know which ingredients you need to shop for and which you need to stockpile. This will help increase your savings because you are going to have the ingredients you need in your stockpile, paying rock bottom for those items versus paying retail at the store. If you are already saving 50 to 70 percent on your groceries and you start monthly menu planning, you will see additional savings as well.

If you plan monthly menus, we suggest including one family favorite meal each week and including a leftovers night each week. By including a family favorite, you are assured that at least one night a week everyone will be looking forward to a meal. We often mention that night when we serve a meal that not everyone loves. For example, at our houses, every Sunday is "Brinner"—breakfast for dinner! Our kids love it! Also, every Friday is make your own pizza night at our houses, another huge hit on our menu plan. Melissa has Taco Tuesday night at her house, which her family loves. By mentioning these nights, we give our children something to look forward to when we are not serving their favorite meals. Label and date leftovers and refrigerate or freeze them. They should be kept for no more than three days. Also, you should reheat only once, so it is best to reheat servings on a plate versus reheating the entire dish. If it is in your budget, you can include dining out weekly or monthly.

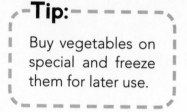

Tip:
Buy vegetables on special and freeze them for later use.

Melissa began using monthly menu planning in 2006 and found it very useful. She introduced Shelley to monthly menu planning in 2009. If you dislike the question, "What's for dinner tonight?" you will love monthly menu planning. It really eliminates that question because you know what is for dinner every night! It also decreases your dining out expense because you are less likely to be tempted to stop and pick up something on your way home or order takeout. You will already have your meal prepared or ready to be prepared. We find it is a huge budget saver.

To add flexibility to your menu planning, try flipping the days if necessary. If something comes up in the week, then you have that option. Be sure to include a variety of foods in your menu plan. We like to include one food from every food group. We center our meal plan on the protein (beans, chicken, beef, turkey, pork) and build from that. We choose the protein based on what is on sale, what we find on manager's special, or what is in our freezer. A great way to save money from your budget is to skip canned beans and buy dried beans in bulk. It is a frugal way to add protein to your family's diet. By buying dried beans in bulk and soaking them overnight, you can add protein to your menu plan. It is also the healthiest way to go since canned beans usually contain lots of sodium and preservatives. Dried beans are very cheap and expand when soaked, so you get more for your money! Be sure to remove any small rocks or pebbles before soaking. Add three times more water than beans, soak over-night, and then prepare the next day. You can also keep these in a storage bag in your refrigerator or freezer. Simply date them and place them in the freezer.

Spices are a great way to add flavor to recipes. Save money by using spices you and your family like to add flavor to inexpensive cuts of meat. Pasta and canned tomatoes are also inexpensive foods to add to your menu plan. You can really stretch your budget by choosing a recipe with pasta, rice, potatoes, or beans as the main ingredient. Then add a smaller amount of meat or vegetables. Another stockpiling tip is to purchase vegetables like onions and peppers on manager's special and then freeze them to use later. When you eliminate meat as the main focus of your meal, you will see the savings in your family budget.

We include a variety of textures, shapes, colors, and temperatures in our menu plan. Use the food guide pyramid (MyPyramid .gov) as your guide. You can also go to ChooseMyPlate.gov, which recommends you fill half your plate with vegetables, a quarter with protein, and the last quarter with whole grains. To get started, write down all of the meals that you know how to prepare and your family likes to eat. If that list is not very long, then you may want to consider looking for quick and frugal recipes. We like recipes with five ingredients or fewer because they are typically frugal and simple to prepare. Serve soups, casseroles, or one-pot meals to further stretch your budget. CookingWithStockpilingMoms.com is a family-friendly foodie blog dedicated to helping you save time in the kitchen. We feature recipes, menu planning and kitchen tips and tricks that make household management easier. Another great resource for finding frugal recipes is AFewShortcuts.com. Also check out MomsWithCrockpots.com and PocketChangeGourmet .com. After you have your list, it is easy to fill up the calendar with what you know how to cook.

> **Tip:**
>
> Visit CookingWith StockpilingMoms .com for more tips.

We use a magnetic dry erase calendar on our refrigerator to plan our menus. This allows everyone in the family to know what is for dinner. It keeps us accountable to follow our menu plan, and since the kitchen is grand central station in our homes, it keeps us organized. Another idea would be to keep a paper calendar hanging in your kitchen. It is also nice to keep a copy in your coupon binder. By planning menus monthly, you are able to know what ingredients you need to stockpile. This will decrease your dining out and grocery expenses.

Another idea is to consider bulk or batch cooking and freezing meals. It will save you time and is especially helpful if you work outside of the home or have a busy schedule. You can really extend your stockpile by freezer cooking. We didn't think we were ever busy enough to consider freezer cooking until now. Between blogging and being a wife, mother, chauffeur, assistant soccer coach, PTO, and the list goes on and on, we just don't have the time to cook like we used to. Having home-cooked meals every night is very important to us, so freezer cooking is a good option that helps save us both time and money.

Taking the idea of monthly menu planning to batch cooking, or once a month cooking, is not a huge change. What it means is that you will spend one to two full days cooking and prepare twenty meals so that your family has dinner "ready" every day. All you have to do is put the dish in the oven and add side dishes, and your dinner is ready.

There are a couple of ways to try it. You can double your recipes or even triple them and repeat the same dish multiple times in the month. You can prepare a large quantity of meats or vegetables and use them in a variety of dishes. We personally decided to look at the recipes that our family likes to eat and what we thought would freeze well. Of course, in order to do this, you need freezer space, and we suggest investing in a food saver (or freezer bags or containers). It is also very important to label and date your food before placing it into the freezer.

In order to be successful, you need to be organized. We suggest shopping one day for ingredients that are not in your stockpile, prepare one day, and cook and clean up the third day. It is nice to recruit help when you begin the process. If you have an assistant to help with preparing and cooking as well as clean-up, then it won't be as overwhelming. Another stockpiling tip is to start out small. Try cooking one to two weeks's worth of meals the first time and then gradually increase to a month. A helpful freezer cooking tip: Do not freeze meals with mayonnaise or sour cream. They don't freeze well. Here is a sample plan for twenty meals.

Meatloaf: Double
Homemade Marinara: Triple
Pancakes: Triple
Chicken Casserole: Double
Lasagna: Double
Chicken Enchiladas: Double
Stuffed Pork Chops: Triple
Burgers: Triple

A great resource for once a month cooking is OnceAMonth Mom.com. Most important, if you decide to try freezer cooking, have fun! This truly needs to be a day that you devote to cooking all day. Clean up as you go and ask for help; it doesn't have to be a one-person job. Crank up your favorite music and, though it is a lot of work, just think about the benefits. You will have dinner prepared for the next month!

Dinnertime Is Family Time

Mealtime is a very important time for our families. We dedicate our evening dinner time as "precious family time." We eat at the dinner table, and we don't allow TV, phones, or toys. This is something that we feel very strongly about. For us, dinnertime is an important time to reconnect during the day, and it allows us to have thirty to forty-five minutes of uninterrupted time together. If you are not eating dinner together as a family, we encourage you to consider it.

Have children participate in and take responsibility for dinner. Melissa's son sets the table while she finishes preparing dinner, and then when her husband gets home, they sit down for their meal. Her son has been setting the table since he was four! He actually asked if he could. At first she helped him, but now he has it down to a science. He likes to put out a fork, spoon, and knife with a napkin at every meal. Regardless of whether they are using all the utensils, she thinks it is important to teach the value of setting the table correctly, so she always allows him to do it. Sometimes he asks if they can use stemmed glasses, and she always agrees. Allowing him to participate in setting the table gives him ownership in dinner. It also teaches him responsibility.

Melissa likes to keep dinnertime early at her house because their schedule allows it. They normally have dinner ready no later than 5:30. If her husband is going to be late, then they fix him a plate to eat later. However, there are very few nights that he doesn't make it home. Shelley's family eats dinner later, so she prepares her boys a later afternoon snack to tide them over until dinner. Regardless of your family's schedule, you can make family dinnertime work for you.

During dinner, we have simple conversation. This is something that keeps the communication lines open. It is very important that everyone sit in his or her own chair while we eat and stay seated for the entire meal. We wait for everyone to finish before we get up to work on the dishes, and it is every person's responsibility to clear his or her own place at the table, again, teaching responsibility. Now, when it comes to eating, we have a rule that you must "try" every item that is prepared. Particularly if you have a picky eater, then the one-bite rule may work for you. Another idea is that your child may have to eat as many bites as their age. This is just a suggestion. If you start with this rule, then it is something your children will be used to as they get older.

6

drugstores

If you are paying for health and beauty products, you shouldn't be. One thing that we don't like to pay for is anything that goes down the drain. With that said, you should not be paying for shampoo, body wash, soap, shaving cream, razors, and much more! If you play the drug store games, as we like to call it, then you can stockpile most health and beauty aids and over-the-counter medicine for free or near free.

Every single week, the three major drugstores offer products free after coupons and incentives. By playing the drugstore games, you can walk out of the store week after week with cheap and free products. Each of the three major drugstores has its own incentive program and coupon policy. What we suggest is that you target the free products each week to really bring down your out-of-pocket expenses for health and beauty aids. If you play the drugstore games, you should be able to almost entirely eliminate health and beauty aids and over-the-counter medications from your budget.

We suggest comparing all three of the major drugstores' coupon policies, and depending on which you have available to you, determine which you will utilize most. Compare distance, policies, and incentives, and that will help make your decision. Please note that coupon policies are changing all of the time, so it is important to ask your store for their coupon policy before you start playing the drugstore games. Oftentimes people think that shopping at drugstores is expensive, when in reality, it is about strategic coupon use. If you play the games, you can save big!

Walgreens

We like shopping at Walgreens even though you have to really think through your shopping trip to get the most for your money. Walgreens does not double coupons. They do allow you to stack one manufacturer coupon and one store coupon per item; however, you must purchase a total amount of items that equal the same number of coupons redeemed. This means that if you use nine coupons, you must purchase nine items. If you stack coupons, you will need to place a "filler" item in your cart. So for example, if you purchase one item and use both a store coupon and a manufacturer's coupon, you will have to add one "filler" item to the transaction so that the coupons don't beep. They offer Instant Value Coupons (IVC) each week, which are located in their sales ads and in-store. They also have a Register Rewards (RR) program. An RR is a Catalina coupon that prints out after you have purchased a qualifying item.

An RR will expire two weeks from the date issued, and they *won't* accept an expired RR. If you use an RR to purchase an item from a like brand (or a brand in the same family), another RR will not print. You cannot make a purchase with an RR and get another RR to print, meaning that an RR will not "roll." An RR can be earned only once per transaction. If you want to earn more than one, you will need to make multiple transactions and not pay with the RR that printed from the same *brand* or family of brands product. This requires you to keep your brands straight when it comes to using an RR to pay for an item that produces an RR. This is what we meant when we said it requires you to really think through your shopping trip.

You will need to invest about $10 when you start shopping at Walgreens. We personally target the free after RR items each week and always try to walk out of the door with at least $10 of RR.

In order to get your total down to the lowest amount possible and for the register to accept all of your coupons, the order you give your coupons is very important. Walgreens cashiers normally will not manually force a coupon through. So if your coupon beeps, they will just hand it back to you. Also, be sure to hand your coupons over in the following order to get the least out-of-pocket expense. Hand over Register Rewards first, followed by manufacturer coupons, and store coupons last. If you are checking out and a coupon beeps, and you know it is a valid coupon, try adding an additional filler item and see if your coupon works. It is a good idea to target filler items prior to check out; we suggest checking the clearance aisle or purchasing an inexpensive sucker or pack of gum. These could be used as treats for your children.

If for some reason the cashier cannot get a coupon to go through, request that they void the item off of your order. It's much easier to just void it off and not pay for it, then to return it later. Also, do not be afraid to walk away from a transaction if it doesn't go your way; however, be sure to take your coupons with you. Always ask for a store manager if you have problems with your order or an RR doesn't print.

We also suggest checking out at the beauty counter. Oftentimes they have an additional coupon or offer for you to use. We find that by checking out at the beauty counter, we are able to do multiple transactions because we are not slowing down the main cash register. Walgreens also offers money off store coupons; however, these normally state that they must be used after all manufacturer and store coupons. Be sure to read the wording on your coupons. Walgreens also offers friends and family discounts, where you can get an additional percentage off of your total purchase. These are great discounts that you can combine with your coupons. Be sure to sign up for email offers at Walgreens.com. In general, you can have great success at Walgreens if you follow these guidelines. It just takes a little bit of careful planning and counting of items to match coupons used, and it can be worth your planning. Each week at StockpilingMoms.com, we provide a detailed Walgreens matchup for you.

CVS

CVS has a fabulous incentive system, and if you use it to your advantage, you will walk away with free products each and every week. If you work the CVS system to your advantage, you will not pay for any health or beauty item or most over-the-counter medication. They do not double coupons but they do allow you to stack manufacturer and store coupons. They also have a store loyalty program (Extra Care Card), and you can sign up for one per person in your household. Our advice is to never shop at CVS without this card because all of the sales and incentives are linked to your Extra Care Card. You can pick one up from the cashier before checking out and use it immediately. Be sure to link your card to your email account so that you can get their email updates, many of which include valuable coupons that can be stacked with a store and manufacturer coupon. Oftentimes CVS will provide mail-in rebate offers that net free after rebate. The form prints at the register immediately upon purchase.

Always hand your CVS card to the cashier first, before they ring up a single item. This allows for you to get credit and the correct sale prices. At CVS, you can earn Extra Care Bucks (ECB) based on your purchases and Extra Care Coupons (ECQ), which print at the bottom of your receipt. ECBs have an expiration date of one month from the date they are printed, and they are the same as cash. If you were to find an expired ECB, they will normally allow you to use it for up to thirty days after the expiration date; however, ask your store manager for approval. We find this to be the same for ECQ.

You must have your Extra Care Card to redeem your ECB and ECQ. This is important to know because you cannot give your ECB or ECQ to another person to use; they are linked to your card. You will have to pay sales tax, when applicable, when redeeming an ECB. Make sure you use your ECB from highest to lowest in value because they will not allow you to use ECB to pay for sales tax. It may become necessary to add a filler item to bring your total above the value of your ECB in order to redeem them.

If you work the CVS program, you will be able to walk out the door with free merchandise and normally make money while doing so. By using a manufacturer or store coupon, you will often be able to make money on your transactions. Oftentimes, you can even match them with a mail-in rebate. Also, always scan your CVS card at the coupon kiosk at your local CVS store to see if you have any special offers or coupons available. They will print out at the kiosk instantly. If you scan your card more than once at the coupon kiosk, you may get additional coupons.

You will need to invest money the first time you shop at CVS to start the process. What you are going to do is target items that produce an ECB. Every week, there are several items that are free after ECB, and you want to purchase those items. You are actually earning the same amount or sometimes more than what you are paying for the item in ECBs. You can find out what items produce ECBs by looking in the CVS sales circular or on StockpilingMoms .com. At CVS, you can "roll" your ECBs earned toward a purchase that produces ECBs. So your objective is to purchase an item with ECBs that you will earn additional ECBs for, meaning you can pay for an item with ECBs and earn ECBs at the same time. This system will allow you to spend the least out of pocket, and if worked correctly, after your first investment you are going to pay very little on all of your future shopping trips. You will still have to pay sales tax, if applicable.

Also, you can earn ECBs by using the Green Bag Tag program. You can purchase the Green Bag Tag for $0.99 at your local store. To earn ECBs for a transaction at your store, your Extra Care Card, Green Bag Tag, and a reusable bag must be presented when you make your purchase at the checkout. One Green Bag Tag use per day per Extra Care Card is allowed. For every fourth purchase, a $1 ECB will print at the bottom of your cash register receipt. This can be redeemed for any additional purchases. It is a great way to earn extra ECBs and help the environment.

It is important to link your card to your email address and mailing address so that you can receive valuable money-off store coupons. These coupons can be combined with manufacturer coupons, and unlike Walgreens coupons, they apply to your real total rather than your pre-coupon total. In addition, occasionally you will get a free product coupon and other special offers. Always hand the cashier your CVS Extra Care Card followed by your store coupons, then ECBs, and finally any manufacturer coupons. This will get you the least out-of-pocket expense. Each week at StockpilingMoms.com we provide a detailed CVS matchup for you.

Rite Aid

Rite Aid is another great resource for decreasing your budget. They do not double coupons. However, they offer a Single Check Rebate (SCR) program. In the SCR program, you purchase qualifying items and then submit them for a rebate at the end of the month. You can stack SCR items with manufacturer and store coupons as well as their various other incentive programs. The SCR checks come in the form of an actual check in the mail, not something that needs to be redeemed again at their store.

Like the other drugstores, you will have to invest some money into the program before you start earning your SCR checks. After you submit for your SCR, you can use that money to continue making purchases to help lower any out of pocket expenses. If you purchase qualifying items, they will send you additional coupon savings books in the mail. Several items each week are free after SCR. You can find the "free after SCR" items listed in the sales curricular. If you have coupons that match SCR items, then they will become moneymakers for you!

You can sign up for the SCR program at your local Rite Aid store. You do have to keep your receipts and enter them into your account after your shopping trip. We suggest placing them into a small accordion folder or entering them into your account after each shopping trip. Rite Aid also offers an +UP Rewards (UPR) program, which gives you special coupons earned by a customer in a prior purchase that can be used for any nonprescription purchase (with a small number of exclusions that are listed on the +UP coupon). Multiple +UP coupons can be used (subject to the printed exclusions) up to the amount of the purchase before sales tax. The +UP Rewards also roll, similar to the CVS ECB program.

They also offer coupons from watching videos at riteaid.adperk .com. After you watch the video, you can print a Video Value coupon that you can redeem at the store. In addition, they offer a Wellness+ card. Be sure to link your current address and email address to your Wellness+ card. This is a great way to get additional money-saving offers. Each Tuesday at StockpilingMoms.com, we provide a "best of Rite Aid" matchup for you in our Stockpile Time post.

7

budget

If you don't have a family budget, you may be very surprised by how much you are actually spending. If you live by a detailed budget, you will hold yourself accountable for all of your spending. You will be able to get a handle on your expenses. In order to see how much you are saving from stockpiling you will want to create a budget, at least for groceries. We believe in living by a budget so that you can see where you're spending and start saving as well.

How to Create a Family Budget—The first step in living a disciplined and financially healthy life is to create a family budget. It can't be for just you or your spouse; it must be for the entire family, including effectively managing little Johnny's or Suzie's monthly toy budget. A family budget is a great tool to assist your family in meeting both short- and long-term goals, whether it's paying down debt, being able to afford a child's private education, planning for retirement, or even saving for a vacation home.

Gather All Your Financial Statements—This includes bank statements, investment accounts, recent utility bills, and any other sources of information related to income or expenses. The objective is to gain a better understanding of your family's cash flow.

Record All of Your Income—If your income comes in the form of a regular paycheck, in which taxes are automatically deducted, it is fine to use the net amount, or take-home pay amount.

If you are self-employed or have other sources of income (for example, rental property and so on), record those sources as well.

Make a List of Monthly Expenses—Now make a list of all expected expenses you will incur each month. This includes fixed and variable expenses, which can be categorized as discretionary and nondiscretionary expenses. This could include mortgage payments, car payments, utilities expenses, insurance payments, school loan payments, grocery purchases, dining out, retirement or college savings, and essentially anything that you spend money on.

Compare Income and Expenses—After compiling a list of your sources of income and monthly expenses, it's now time to compare your results. If you have more income than expenses, then you're off to a good start. Now you can focus your excess to areas of your budget such as an emergency fund, retirement savings, college savings, or a vacation home. If you are spending more than you bring home, then you may be using credit to cover the "shortfall" and will need to make some changes.

Target Discretionary Expenses and Start Cutting Down—If you have accurately identified and listed all your expenses, the ultimate goal would be to have your income and expense columns be equal, which means all of your income is accounted for and directed for specific expenses, including savings.

If you're spending more than you're bringing in, then you need to start with discretionary expenses to find areas to cut. With discretionary expenses, it should be easy to trim some money in a few areas to bring your expenses closer to your income.

Start Prioritizing Your Debts—If you have debts (for example, credit cards), your budget should already include the minimum payments that you have to make each month; however, you need to find money to pay down those debts. Start with the account with the highest interest rate. Pay that debt off, and then go to the next most costly account.

Use the budget template provided at StockpilingMoms.com to create your own family budget.

Track Your Expenses—Each week, we spend fifteen minutes or so "updating the books," or tracking our expenses, by updating Quicken. We've found it much less daunting to spend a few minutes each week to record expenses instead of updating in one large chunk of time. After the first month, it's important to compare your actual expenses to your budgeted amount to make sure you're staying on track. This will highlight where you did well and other areas where you may need to tweak your budget.

Keep It Real, Stick with It, and Tweak Your Budget—It is absolutely critical to keep your budget realistic and stick with it. If you didn't meet your goal, try to figure out why you weren't able to stay on budget. Did you set an unrealistic goal? Or was there an anomaly or unexpected event? We review our budget each month. If we don't, then we may lose sight of any "leakage" and not stay on track to ensure we meet our financial goals.

Finally, during our annual benefits enrollment window (October/November timeframe), we take the opportunity to draft the next year's budget by leveraging the existing year's budget. Overall, most line items remain true; however, we may have some expected expenses in the coming year that we need to include within the budget. Additionally, we'll review the prior year's budget results and make any necessary changes by lowering or expanding an expense category.

Tips and Suggestions

1. Debt reduction should be Priority #1.
2. To save yourself some grief, use a personal finance software program such as Quicken or Microsoft Money, which offer built-in budgeting tools.
3. We are believers in the notion, "the devil is in the details." Don't be overzealous in tracking expenses, and shift your focus to expense categories. You don't need a line item for expenses in which you spend less than $100 per year.
4. Avoid cash leakage, ATM withdrawals, and bank fees—If you use cash to pay for expenses, it's critical to track and categorize your cash expenses.
5. Obviously, when the US economy crashed in the fourth quarter of 2008, a contributing factor was the fact that many Americans were "living outside their means" by spending

beyond their limits and relying on credit accounts. Don't let this happen to you.

6. Shoot for spending only 90 percent of your income and allocate the remaining 10 percent to big-ticket items, like retirement savings, college savings, an emergency fund, a vacation home, and so on.

7. Be patient and don't get frustrated. It will take you three to four months before you get better with your budgeting.

8. Don't include sources of income that you can't be sure you'll receive like investment gains, tax refunds, and so on.

9. Even though your income may increase over time due to annual salary increases, promotions, or smart investing, don't start spending on luxury items until you're sure you've covered inflation. For example, I received a 2 percent merit increase in 2010; however, tax breaks expired at the end of 2010, so our effective tax bracket increased by 3 percent, resulting in having less disposable income in 2011.

These tips and suggestions should help guide you as you create your budget. If you are not tech-savvy, don't let that stop you from saving money. You can always create your budget on pen and paper. We are huge believers in living by a detailed budget. We have for the past six years, and at first it was an eye-opening experience for us. It was a way for us to get a handle on our spending and eliminate frivolous spending and credit card debt.

8

dining out

Do you love to eat out? We do! However, as we mentioned in chapter 7, we live by a very strict budget, and that includes our dining out budget too! Melissa budgets $200 a month for dining out. This includes every meal that they eat out. Melissa's husband does not eat out during the week. He packs his lunch every day and therefore that does not affect their dining out budget. That $200 a month includes all expenses for occasional date nights too. If you don't have a budget, again, we stress that you should. At a minimum, if you have created a grocery budget, we suggest creating a dining out budget too. You may want to consider using a cash envelope method for dining out because it will help you stick to your budget. When your dining out envelope is empty, that means no more dining out until the next month. You will not be tempted to overspend by placing charges for meals on your credit card.

There are lots of great ways to save when it comes to dining out. Our first dining out tip is to join e-clubs linked to local restaurants. They often offer coupons and birthday offers too! It is a great way to eat at half price or even free! Another suggestion is to share an entrée when you are getting a free appetizer (with coupon) from an e-club offer. Always drink water. Paying for a soft drink when dining out is as expensive as

Tip:

Join e-clubs linked to local restaurants to eat out for less.

a twelve pack, so drinking water is a major budget saver. Another way to save on your budget is to look for restaurants that offer free dining for kids. Consider going out to lunch when it is more affordable and less crowded. Plus lunch portions are more reasonable in size. We also suggest becoming a mystery shopper at SecretShopper .com. This is a great way to eat out while not affecting your budget! Another suggestion is to purchase gift cards to your favorite merchants for up to 60 percent off at sites such as plasticjungle.com and giftcardgranny.com.

Additional tips to save while dining out include

- Use Cheap Tweets—CheapTweets.com.
- Check 2chambers.com for discounts.
- Utilize credit card and bank rewards.
- Check for AAA discounts—AAA.com

We also suggest purchasing an entertainment book. It is a great resource for discounts when dining out. Consider purchasing one for your vacation destination too. Sometimes these books are even sold at half price! The offers can be used at restaurants, movies, and some entertainment venues. You have to carry it with you to use it, so if your entertainment book is at home, you won't be able to save! We suggest keeping it in your car. We keep ours in the backseat pocket and take it with us everywhere we go. This is a great way to try new restaurants too!

You can also purchase deeply discounted gift certificates to local restaurants at Restaurant.com. You can sign up at Restaurant.com for email offerings, and they will send you discount codes. Oftentimes you can purchase them at 80 percent off! Please make sure you read the fine print on the offers before you purchase them. There are often limits that you can use only one Restaurant.com gift certificate per table. Often they will require you to make some sort of additional purchase as well. For example, a $25 gift certificate may only be used on a $35 or more meal. For legal reasons, you cannot use gift certificates toward alcohol. In addition, some restaurants will limit the days of the week they can be used. Shelley uses Restaurant.com gift certificates often, and it really brings her dining out budget down. This is a great way to think outside of the box when it comes to dining out. Just always be sure to read the fine print.

Daily deal sites are another way to get huge discounts while discovering new places to eat in your city. Each day they feature a new offer at an unbeatable price in dozens of cities across the country. They can be a great way to save from your family budget. Again, it is really important to read the fine print and expiration date on the offers. Remember it is only a deal if you use it! We have taken advantage of many daily deals in our city. Oftentimes you will earn a bonus into your account when you sign up. We suggest signing up for daily email updates so you don't miss out on the offers that interest you. Some daily deal sites include Groupon.com, LivingSocial.com, Tippr.com, CouponDealsDaily.com, and EverSave.com. However, there are so many new daily deal sites popping up every day.

Don't forget bonus gift card deals when they're available around the holidays because that can really save your family's dining out budget. If you dine out, you may want to take advantage of these deals for your budget! Each year we purchase gift cards to restaurants we love and taking advantage of the free bonus gift cards during the holidays. Also, if you are paying with a credit card, be sure to use one where you can earn cash back for your purchases. Also be sure to read the fine print and check for expiration dates when purchasing bonus gift cards. Make sure to use them before they expire and look for limitations if any.

Another resource is Upromise.com. Upromise is a program that allows you to build a college fund for anyone you choose. After registering, simply present your Upromise card at checkout every time you shop at participating stores and restaurants. Many store loyalty cards can be linked directly to your account. Every time you make an eligible purchase, the partners return a portion of that money back to you. Those earnings accumulate in your Upromise account until you decide to use it to invest in a 529 plan, help pay down eligible student loans, or assist with college expenses, all tax-free! It is not a coupon but a college savings program. In addition, they offer e-coupons. When you purchase an item, the e-coupon amount gets deposited into your account. They also offer special dining out offers and discounts, online shopping incentives and discounts, and more. If you don't have children, you can save for other children in your life. You can sign up for free at Upromise.com.

You can also save by downloading apps to use with your smartphone. They are often free and are a great way to save money. We suggest using Foursquare. Many retailers post exclusive deals on this location-based app. When you "check in" online at a restaurant or store and a deal pops up on your phone, show your screen to the cashier to get the offer. This is available for Android, BlackBerry, iPhone, Ovi Nokia, Palm, and more. Another great app is WeReward. Earn points as you complete tasks at local shops and restaurants and then trade your points for cash. This is available for Android, BlackBerry, and iPhone. If you have a smartphone, we really suggest taking time to look at apps that can help save you money. More apps continue to appear every day.

9

healthy couponing

It is a misconception that you cannot both eat healthy and use coupons. In 2010, we lost a combined total of sixty-five pounds and stayed within our monthly grocery budgets! You have to think outside of the box when it comes to healthy couponing, but it is possible. We want to share with you several tips for healthy couponing success. First, continue to play the drugstore games. As we mentioned in chapter 6, you can really take advantage of freebies on health and beauty aids as well as over-the-counter medications from playing the drugstore games. Second, continue to clip coupons for basic staples and household items. This will continue to save you 50 to 70 percent every time you shop.

A healthy couponing tip is to take advantage of manager's specials. Every day, reductions are made in all departments, especially produce, dairy, and meat departments, with manager's specials. Utilize your freezer to extend the life of the manager's specials. We always purchase our fruits and vegetables on manager's special and incorporate them into our menu plan. Typically, you can pick up manager's specials every single day. We suggest shopping early to get the best variety of manager's specials. By incorporating those into your meal plan, you will be able to save big on perishables.

Our biggest healthy couponing tip is, don't clip coupons for junk food. If you clip the coupon, then you will be tempted to purchase it. If you purchase it, you will be tempted to eat it. This is a

> **Tip:**
>
> For healthier eating, don't clip coupons for junk food.

great way to eliminate those foods from your diet. If you don't clip those coupons, you won't purchase them and won't eat them.

When we started our healthy lifestyle, Shelley purged all of the junk food from her stockpile and donated it to charity. You could donate it to your local food bank, homeless shelter, or other nonprofit association. Most of the unhealthy items she gave away did not cost her much, if anything at all. To better her life, she knew she had to get rid of it. Taking a moment to reevaluate and donate from your stockpile may be necessary if you make the decision to eat healthier.

Another suggestion is to price match when possible. Some stores allow you to bring a current competitor's sale ad into the store, and they will "match" that price. This allows you to make fewer trips and shop at a store that is conveniently located to you. Stores that price match include Walmart and Target. To price match, you must have an original sales curricular with current date; it cannot be an internet print-out of the sale items. This useful tool helps reduce your out-of-pocket costs, and another benefit to price matching is that you will save time because you won't have to drive to additional stores. We also factor in our decision to price match if a store allows overage.

Another stockpiling tip is to utilize overage. If your store allows it, then use the overage to put healthy items in your cart. This is a great way to save on the products that don't typically offer coupons. For example, we like to use overage to save on organic products, fruit, vegetables, eggs, meat, and dairy. When you purchase an item for $0.75 and use a coupon for $1, you are "over" $0.25 on the item and can earn money back toward other items in your order. Some stores, however, will automatically adjust the amount of the coupon "down" to match the price of the product. Other stores, like Walmart and often Kroger, will allow you to earn and use the overage. Target and Family Dollar oftentimes give overage too. We want to mention, however, that "your mileage may vary" (YMMV) when it comes to overage. Unless the official coupon policy states that you earn overage (like at Walmart), then it may depend on your cashier or register.

Healthy coupons do exist! A variety of websites offer healthy coupons. Our favorite resource is MamboSprouts.com. If you shop for organic products, many organic coupons are available as well. Some great resources include Lifeway.com, SantaCruzOrganic.com, Stoneyfield.com, AlmondBreeze.com, JanesKrazy.com, Michael Angelos.com, OrganicValley.coop, BlueDiamond.com, RiceSelect .com, SeventhGeneration.com, ThinkProducts.com, Snikiddy.com, Naturespath.com, Crunchmaster.com, WholeFoodsMarket.com, and Earthfare.com.

One of the best healthy couponing tips is to check with the brands that you love and see if they offer an e-newsletter or e-club. If you have a brand that you are loyal to or one that you would really like to try, visit their website. They may have online coupons, an e-club, or a rewards program that you didn't know about. If not, simply contact them and request a coupon. The worst that can happen is that they will say no. Often these e-newsletters and e-clubs will include coupons. This is a great way to save on items that you love but that don't offer regular coupons. There are even sometimes coupons for fruit, vegetables, and milk; however, when they are released, they go quickly. For another resource, sign up at Driscolls (http://www.driscolls.com/email/) because they often offer coupons and send you one for your birthday too!

Forming a Co-op

As we mentioned, think outside of the box when it comes to healthy couponing. One way that Melissa saves on produce is by participating in a food co-op. By pooling their money together, members of a food co-op are able to buy produce in bulk and save big. If you have a local produce source available to you, it is easy to form a produce co-op. If you don't have one, then you could contact your local produce manager at your grocery store and ask if you could get a bulk discount and go in that direction. We are lucky to have a produce location available to us where we can purchase wholesale or bulk quantity.

After you figure out your source for purchasing your produce, it is time to form your co-op group. Put out the word to friends and family, and you will be surprised how many you will find are interested. Decide how much you will need to charge each person to participate. In Melissa's co-op, they charge $15 for a "single share" or $30 for a "double share." When it comes to requests, you can take them with the understanding that they may or may not be fulfilled. Some people may be allergic to or dislike certain produce items. However, fulfilling requests can be quite difficult. You can try within reason to fulfill requests, but there should be no guarantee. Melissa's co-op includes both fruit and vegetables, and they purchase one new product each shopping trip to introduce variety to the group. Your co-op could be monthly or bi-monthly depending on what you are interested in.

Melissa's co-op group has two shoppers each month. One is an "experienced shopper" and one is an "inexperienced shopper." This gives the proper training to the inexperienced shopper, and no one person has to do the shopping each month. The shoppers are responsible for bringing boxes or bags, and they are responsible for separating the produce into shares. This works well because it allows each person in the group to learn how to shop, sort, and take their fair turn. Because the market opens at 6:30 a.m. and it takes several hours for the process, it is nice to share the responsibility. The more participants, the better variety you can get for the group because you are able to pool more money. Each member gets equal items in their share. Some food co-ops include www.bountifulbaskets.org, www.localharvest.org, foodcoop.com, www.oklahomafood.coop, and hillsideproducecooperative.org. Check online for potential co-ops in your area.

Another resource for produce is to purchase from your local farmers market. We love to support local farmers and find that we can get a better price from them than at the store. They often have items like honey, herbs, and eggs for sale as well. There are many reasons a farmers market is more beneficial for the environment and economy. Farmers markets strengthen communities and local economies. This helps your money circulate within your own community. It is good for the environment because your food is not traveling as far, so it is not adding to pollution, does not require packaging, and is less intensively grown. Because you have fewer miles on your food, it can also reduce the cost.

We have met a lot of really nice people at farmers markets. They are more likely to give you a better price on their products because you are cutting out the middleman. If you want organic crops, you can also look for those at the farmers market, and it is nice to know where your fruits and vegetables are coming from. If you shop at the end of the day, you can often pick up deals and "need to sell quickly" produce. Then take it home and freeze it or use it right away to get the most for your money. Another idea is to go to a local farm to pick your own produce. Go to pickyourown.org to find a farm near you. Both of these are fantastic educational opportunities for your children as well.

Another great way to save on produce is to garden yourself. There is nothing more rewarding than having your own garden. This is a family fun activity that really gets everyone involved regardless of their age because everyone can contribute. You can decide if you want to use pesticides or garden organically. Melissa gardens organically with no pesticides. The first year that you garden, you will have to spend more out of pocket. The first year Melissa gardened, she invested in tomato cages and was lucky to borrow a rotary tiller from her neighbor. In addition to the cost of her plants and seeds, that was about the total of her expenses. She lives on a wooded lot with deer and other pesky rodents, so she had to invest in deer and rodent repellent. However, there are many natural methods to ridding your garden of unwanted pests too. One frugal tip is to collect unwashed hair from the barber and spread it around the outside of your garden. You can also use a dishwashing liquid/water mixture to spray on your plants.

We do want to mention that you don't have to have a large yard or acreage to garden. Regardless of space, you can garden in a small area, within your existing landscaping, or even in pots on your patio or deck. Take the space you have and utilize it by adding a few plants and see where it takes you. Gardening is a fabulous, frugal family activity. We plant together. Then we weed, water, harvest, and eat together. It has been a wonderful way to add fresh vegetables into our menu plan and reduce our family budget.

Another idea is to purchase a cow or pig from a local farmer. You can purchase in bulk and get a better price per pound. Of course, you need to have freezer space when you purchase it. How much meat your family eats will determine how much you will need to purchase. Our suggestion is to start with half a cow and see how long it lasts. You will find that the meat has less fat and is higher quality than what you find at the store. You can also request specific cuts of meat and sizes. A great stockpiling tip is to purchase it at tax time after you get your tax return. There is a large cost up front, but it is so worth the savings in the long run!

Not only do you save money, but you also get a much better product for your family (it is usually grass- or corn-fed beef and often hormone- and antibiotic-free). Just ask around for a local cattle farmer and get references from friends. It has less fat and a better taste, can be processed and packaged to your specifications to minimize waste, and has the bonus of supporting a local farmer! Rarely is there anything to drain from farm ground beef after browning it. We have never heard anyone complain once they purchased a side of beef or pig.

If you don't have the freezer space to handle a half, ask a friend or family member if they would like to split a half with you. In that case, you'll both have to agree to have it processed and packaged the same way, but you will both get cuts from both ends of the half. Sometimes farmers (and processors) have other customers only wanting a quarter of a beef that they can match you up with. This is a great way to be able to purchase from a local farmer without having to invest in an additional freezer.

By utilizing these ideas and suggestions, you will realize that healthy coupons do exist; you just have to look a little harder for them.

Losing Weight

We also wanted to share with you some general strategies to lose weight. These are some techniques that we used to lose our sixty-five pounds. However, you should always consult with your doctor before you start a weight-loss plan. We suggest that you exercise three to five days a week. That is easier said than done. Our suggestion is to get dressed in the morning in your workout clothes and shoes. If you are dressed and ready, you are more likely to actually work out. Also, schedule your exercise into your calendar. If it is written down, you will be more likely to do it. Consider getting up an hour earlier and working out before you get ready for your day. You are more likely to work out in the morning, and as a result, you will boost your metabolism and have more energy all day long. Consider adding a two-minute sprint to your workouts. On days you don't have time to work out, consider just doing the two-minute sprint. It will help speed your weight loss.

Fill half of your plate with vegetables. Also consider switching to a salad plate instead of a full-size dinner plate. Limit the amount of processed food you eat or eliminate it altogether and eat only whole foods. Increase your protein and cut back on refined carbohydrates. Be sure to start your day out right by eating breakfast. We encourage you to consider making breakfast your largest meal of the day and then eating a medium-sized meal for lunch and a small meal for dinner. Also be sure to add in healthy snacks between. This will keep your blood sugar regulated, and you will find yourself less hungry at mealtime. Another suggestion is to give up all soft drinks. We eliminated them from our diets. Drink 0.5 ounces of water per pound of your actual body weight a day. Measure out your water each day and drink it before you allow yourself anything else to drink. You can add lemon or lime juice to the water for flavoring. Avoid all fried food and fast food. Set a short-term weight loss goal for yourself and reward yourself when you meet it. Another suggestion is to increase sleep and reduce stress. By doing so, you will find the weight will come off easier.

10

living "naturally" frugal

Another way to save money is to live naturally frugal. There are so many things you can eliminate from your life to help you save money. Hopefully, if you don't already use some of these ideas, you can easily and quickly implement a few to save yourself some money while keeping Mother Earth happy. We have been making several changes in the past year to be "green" and eco-friendly. We wanted to share some of our naturally frugal living ideas with you. Not only does living green teach our children how to be more eco-friendly, it also saves us lots of money!

Our number one suggestion is to avoid using paper plates, plastic flatwear, paper napkins, paper towels, and paper or plastic cups. Not only is it not "green," it also wastes a lot of money that you could be saving. Invest in a stock of reusable plastic plates and cups as well as fabric napkins and hand towels to use instead. This will take some adjusting too, but it is a huge money and environment saver! You may like the ease of paper goods, but in the end, they cost your family a lot of money every year.

As we mentioned in chapter 9, plant a garden. You can also learn to can your own produce. Not only is this a great family activity, there is nothing better than harvesting and eating your own produce. Another idea is to make your own cleaners. You can use diluted white vinegar or baking soda to clean. You can also add natural oils like lavender to scent them. This costs pennies to clean your house! You can also consider making your own laundry detergent. A great recipe is the following:

Use equal parts Borax, washing soda, and baking soda. Use two tablespoons per load. Add two capfuls of bleach to each load and fill the rinse dispenser with white vinegar. This recipe was given to us by our reader Sue Taylor; it works great and costs much less!

Another tip is to start recycling. A benefit of recycling is a reduction in the amount of "garbage," thus reducing the number of garbage bags. Contact your local waste management company and request a recycling bin to recycle paper, plastic, and glass. Most local utilities have recycling services included in your annual waste management expenses or city taxes. Even if you do have to pay for it, it is a great family project, what with sorting items into the bins. It is a great educational tool too. This is a great way to teach your children how to count and responsibility in doing chores, and it saves Mother Earth.

Start composting. If you are gardening, build a compost bin and compost your coffee grounds, eggshells, and fruit and vegetable skins. This will add nutrients to your garden and save space in your garbage. We started composting three years ago, and this year, we were able to work our compost into our garden, which is fabulous natural fertilizer.

Another suggestion is to install an electronic programmable thermostat. Use an electronic thermostat that offers multiple settings for each day of the week. If no one is home during the workday, adjust the setting by five degrees of the desired setting (higher in the summer and lower in the winter) until someone is expected to get home. It is a huge money saver. Consider changing to energy-saving fluorescent lightbulbs. We have gradually switched over to fluorescent lightbulbs, which advertise a longer life and use only 25 percent the energy incandescent bulbs use. Often you can find these for free after rebate or coupon, which is a great time to stockpile.

When shopping for new appliances, look for Energy Star products. They may have a slightly higher purchase price, but you'll save in the long run by using less energy. It can really help reduce your electric bills. Install solar film on windows and use cellular shades or thermal window treatments to save on energy. Also keep shades closed during the day. Install energy-saving receptacle weather insulation to your outlets and light switches. Use a hot water heater blanket and turn your hot water heater down. Wrapping up your water heater with an insulated blanket could save you 7 percent in heating costs. Melissa does this for her gas water heater. You should use a blanket that is designed exclusively for water heaters. Also, take your own bags to grocery shop. You can even earn money or discounts at some stores for doing so!

> **Tip:**
>
> Save energy and money by unplugging your appliances when not in use.

Unplug household appliances when not in use. At night in the dark, have you noticed all the little lights on various household appliances and gadgets? We've each had nights when we couldn't sleep, so we thought we would lie down on the sofa to sleep. Well, we still couldn't go to sleep because it was too bright. Just in our family rooms near the TVs, we have at least three components, and each has bright blue, green, and red lights. Guess what? Even though they are turned "off," they are still consuming 50 to 75 percent of the energy required with normal operation. It may not always be feasible to unplug these appliances, but for those items not used daily or while you're on vacation, you should unplug them and get rid of their wasteful "drain." This is free, and it just takes a second.

We've made it a habit to hang our swimsuits and beach towels up outside to dry after swimming. You can hang a clothesline for even more savings. Another tip is to use your dishwasher versus hand washing dishes and make sure your dishwasher is full before running it. It is also important to change your air filter on your forced air conditioner unit every three to four months. The buildup of dust and dirt within the filter will restrict the airflow through the unit, thereby requiring your system to work harder and longer to keep your home cool or warm, which impacts the overall longevity of your unit. Use electrical timers to turn interior or exterior lights on and off at desired times. This will provide additional security and savings.

Keep your showers short and install an energy-efficient shower-head. Also consider adding a timer to reduce the cost of your water bill. By limiting the amount of time each member of your family uses the shower, you can save drastically on your water bill. Shelley bathes her boys together to save even more. Another idea is to consider reusing gift boxes, bags, and ribbons or eliminate bows altogether. We actually tape name tags on the bags so that we can reuse them.

Take clothes that may be too snug or no longer wanted to consignment stores. If items are in good condition and stylish, they can be sold and provide some additional cash. A helpful tip is to launder and store clothing at the end of the season so that it is ready to go to the consignment store when they start taking items for the next season. One store Melissa consigns at accepts only items on hangers, whereas the other accepts them only when neatly folded in a box. For one store, she launders, presses, folds, and packs her boxes at the end of the season and marks her seller number on the outside so they are ready to go when the next season begins. For the other, she launders, presses, hangs (all in the same direction), buttons, and stores the clothing in a guest bedroom closet so they are ready to go as well. By consigning, she is able to make several hundred dollars each year. She uses the money that she earns from consigning as a "bank." She lets it build up and removes it twice a year, once in May for vacation spending money and once in December for Christmas.

Instead of tossing clothes, household items, or any other items that are still functioning, contact a not-for-profit organization to make a donation. Many organizations will come and pick up your items and provide you with a receipt so that you can take a deduction on your annual federal income tax return. And finally, before your local waste management company arrives, put any desirable items out in open view. Our weekly garbage pickup is on Tuesday, so when we have an item that may be of interest to someone, we make sure to get it out to the street at 6 p.m. Monday evening. This allows plenty of time for someone to drive by and see something they may want for themselves before the garbage is picked up.

Sign up for electronic delivery of your financial statements, Explanation of Benefits (EOB) letters, and utility bills. Sign up at www.donotmail.org, a company that allows you to remove your name from junk mail lists.

In addition to providing protection for your car, waxing your car before a road trip will help you improve your fuel efficiency. Having the proper amount of air pressure in your car tires can help you get more miles per gallon. Take a few minutes to de-junk your trunk—the additional weight will negatively impact your fuel efficiency. If you drive a pickup without a bed topper, make sure you drive with your tailgate up. By driving with your tailgate down, you're creating more "down force," or "drag," which will negatively impact your fuel efficiency. Depending on your geographical location, consider using public transportation or carpooling. Ride a motorcycle instead of driving a car . . . or in Melissa's case, going to two wheels means riding a bicycle.

We hope some of these ideas get you thinking about "going green." It is another way for you to add to your family's savings, help the earth, and begin living a more naturally frugal lifestyle. It does take an investment for some, but once you go green, you will see the benefits of how that can help you save some green. We don't suggest trying to implement these ideas all at one time, but set a goal for implementing several each year and see what a difference it can make on your budget and the environment. If you decide to implement some of these ideas, we suggest you check out Recyclebank .com. When you complete a green action, you are rewarded each time you do it! You are then awarded Recyclebank points, which can be used for rewards at local and national retailers and online! It is free to sign up and a great way to reap the rewards for helping Mother Earth.

11

stockpiling for the holidays

Have you started your holiday shopping? A few years after Melissa got married, she began buying for the holidays and other special occasions throughout the year in order to spread out spending and not get "hit" so hard at the start of the year. This is a great way to save money! After starting the process of International Adoption, we had to find a way to save more money, so we began stockpiling our holiday gifts.

The goal of stockpiling is to purchase your items when they hit rock bottom. This applies to gift-giving too. The first step is to reevaluate your gift-giving list. Eliminate as many gifts as possible by telling friends and coworkers that you are unable to exchange with them anymore. Really cut your shopping list down to only family. After you reevaluate, it is important to tell those who you cut why you are no longer going to be giving them a gift. It is not that you don't love them, but due to the economy, you have made the decision to eliminate as many gifts as possible in your efforts to save money. Most likely they will be relieved. It is important to tell everyone, though, so that they don't purchase a gift for you, which would then make you feel obligated to purchase one for them, and the cycle continues.

Next, make a budget for how much you want to spend per person according to the retail value of the item versus how much you actually spend. That means that if you purchase a $50 sweater for $7, the retail value for that item is $50 even though you only spent $7 out of pocket. Keep retail value in mind when gift-giving. If your goal is to purchase a $50 item, then you met your goal with the $7 item and should feel no pressure to spend $50 out of pocket. This is a major change for most people when shopping for items to be given as gifts. The perception of the retail value, not the amount that you paid out of pocket, is important.

You will begin stockpiling for the next year's holidays the day after that holiday. As we come across a rock-bottom deal, we purchase it and stockpile it for gift-giving later in the year or for the next year's holiday. It is important to keep a detailed spreadsheet of what you purchase throughout the year so that you are not overpurchasing. Even though you are getting the items at rock bottom, you can still overspend. One year Melissa stockpiled enough for two years' worth of Christmas, so it is very important to inventory.

Recipient	Gifts	Retail Value	OOP
Mom	Sweater	$100.00	$25.00
Mom	Pants	$10.00	$5.00
Mom	Socks	$15.00	$2.00
Mom Total		$125.00	$32.00
Dad	Towel	$50.00	$45.00
Dad	Firepit	$200.00	$40.00
Dad Total		$250.00	$85.00
Grand Total		$375.00	$117.00

In order to purchase items at rock bottom to use as gifts, you need to not only buy items that are on sale but also use a coupon when possible. When thinking about coupons for gifts, you may have to stretch your mind to include store coupons; however, it is quite surprising how many "toy" coupons exist! You never know

> **Tip:**
>
> Shop year round for the holidays.

when a great sale or clearance will come along. These matched with clearance items mean rock bottom savings! Our stockpiling tip for you is to shop year round for the holidays. You are going to start shopping for next year immediately after the holiday. This includes all holidays. You can purchase supplies for Valentine's Day, Easter, Halloween, and more the week after the holiday and then save them for the next year. Obviously you don't want to purchase items like candy that expire, but other items like cards, stuffed animals, and trinkets can be picked up for up to 90 percent off after the holiday. This is a great way to save money from your gift-giving budget. Another tip is to stockpile back-to-school supplies in July and August to be used for craft projects all year, birthday presents, and even treat bags at birthday parties or school parties. We have given backpacks full of back-to-school supplies as presents, and they also make great Easter gifts too! Again, think outside of the box when you're stockpiling.

Shop the clearance section when it comes to stockpiling for the holidays. Match coupons to clearance items to get the best deal. Stack manufacturer coupons with store coupons when possible.

Many stores offer Christmas in July sales. Most stores put toys on clearance in July to make room for the new toys for the holidays. This is a great time to stockpile! We often purchase at Kmart and Target during their July clearance sales. This is a great time to stockpile for birthdays too! We find that clearance toy sales are also in January, up to 75 percent off. Be sure to monitor the stores because they will start at 25 percent off and increase to up to 75 percent off. Once they are reduced, they normally sell quickly.

Some stores to consider include

Kohl's: We do a lot of our Christmas shopping at Kohl's. They have great toy sales throughout the year, and on top of that, they offer coupons of up to 30 percent off to store credit card holders. Their clearance toys and other items are often up to 90 percent off. Matched with a store discount on top, you can get a rock bottom deal. Kohl's is our favorite store for major savings when it comes to holiday shopping.

You can often earn $10 Kohl's Cash for every $50 you spend. When you have a Kohl's credit card, you will receive percent off coupons at least twelve times a year. These can be used when you earn Kohl's Cash, but the $50 spent is determined after coupons. When you redeem Kohl's Cash, you can't combine that with a coupon; however, any amount over you can. Kohl's also matches competitor prices. Bring a copy of the competitor ad with current date and make sure the ad includes a description of the item. And Kohl's offers rebates too! Sign up for their email list for a $5 off coupon.

Ace Hardware: Offers e-rebates that you can submit online. These are a great way to give gifts for free! Sign up for an Ace rewards card at acehardware.com. You will earn rewards every time you shop. You get 1,000 free points on your first purchase, 10 points for every dollar you spend, and a $5 reward for every 2,500 points earned. You will also get members-only coupons and every day double points on hot items. They offer a free store calendar with monthly coupons, available in-store around the beginning of the year.

Toys R Us: You can use manufacturer coupons and store coupons at Toys R Us. They often offer mail-in rebates and special incentives for purchases. They offer a rewards card program, called Rewards R Us, where you can earn super savings, exclusive benefits, and more! You can do very well when matching toy coupons to clearance sales.

Staples, Office Max, and Office Depot: All three offer reward cards where you can earn special discounts and earn points on your in-store and online spending. They offer mail-in rebates on products and accept manufacturer coupons. You can save a lot when they have deals that match up with coupons and rebates and oftentimes walk away with a moneymaker. Sign up for email coupons and extra savings. We do an Office Supply Roundup post of the best deals each week, posted on Friday at 5:00 p.m. EST.

Dollar General: Accepts manufacturer coupons and IPs. If you have five coupons for five products, you may use them in one transaction unless the coupon states otherwise. If the coupon states that it is good for any product, you may use the coupon for any product even if it is not pictured, unless the coupon states otherwise.

You may use a Dollar General coupon along with a manufacturer coupon for the same item as long as neither coupon states otherwise. To sign up for Dollar General promotional discounts and offers, visit www.dollargeneral.com and click on the "Email Signup" link at the top of the page. It is a great place to save up to 90 percent off after holiday sales!

Family Dollar: Accepts manufacturer coupons; however, they do not accept IPs or expired coupons. They do accept unlimited coupons. You can't stack two coupons for one item, but you can use store coupons for money off a purchase in combination with manufacturer coupons.

Kmart: They do accept IPs. They do not accept digital coupons. They have a Shop Your Way Rewards card. They do not double coupons except during their double coupon promotion, but they do have rules and restrictions during that promotion. Always check at the customer service desk for their double coupon policy. They also have great clearance sales that make for nice deals when matched with coupons. In July, they have an awesome toy clearance sale (this is where we stock up on birthday and Christmas presents). They offer some incentives for purchasing with them. You can print store coupons from www.kmart.com.

Target: Does not double coupons. You earn $0.05 off your total for each reusable bag that you bring in to use. They do allow you to stack manufacturer and store coupons. They make clearance markdowns weekly, and we suggest asking your store to see which day. They offer special incentives where you earn a free Target gift card for qualifying purchases. The gift card cannot be used on that purchase, but rather on a future purchase. We often break our order into two transactions for the lowest out-of-pocket expense and pay for the second transaction with the gift card earned. They do accept IPs. They do offer rain checks. They do not accept competitor coupons, but they do price match when you bring a competitor ad with you. You can print store coupons from Target.com and at some kiosks in your Target store (where you print off registries). In addition, they offer digital coupons through text alert that you can sign up for online at the Target Mobile Coupon Signup (http://sites .target.com/site/en/spot/mobile_coupon_signup.jsp).

Walmart: Has a new coupon policy that allows overage in the form of earning cash back. Walmart is a great place to use your coupons. Prices don't cycle at Walmart like at other stores because they have everyday low prices. Your best bet is to strategically use your coupons there to earn overage. They also accept IPs and competitor manufacturer coupons (including Catalinas). They do not allow stacking because they do not offer store coupons. They do not offer rain checks, but they do price match. They only accept forty or more coupons, any coupon over $20 in value, or $50 or more in coupons in one transaction with customer service supervisor or management approval.

Thinking Outside of the Box

Think outside of the box when it comes to gift giving. Be creative. Don't forget consignment stores, yard sales, and goodwill. We have picked up items for our children, and though they are not new "in the box," they work well as gifts from Santa. You can really get a lot for your money when goodwill and consignment stores mark down their toys. It is an option that is often overlooked. Consignment stores have clearance sales on their toys to move inventory. Checking at the end of the season is a great time because they need space for the new season's inventory coming in. Check with your goodwill to see if they have a discount day. A helpful stockpile tip is to bring an eraser to test silver items.

We have also been able to fill Christmas stockings for free by skillfully using coupons. Shop the trial size section and match with coupons, and sign up for freebies and samples online! This is a great way to stretch your budget and think outside of the box. Another idea is to earn gift cards from Swag Bucks (Swagbucks.com).

Swag Bucks is not a cash back site but rather a site that allows you to earn great prizes such as iPhones, iPods, concert tickets, gift cards, and more just for using them to search the Internet. Why not get paid for something you are doing anyway? Swag Bucks is powered by Google. In addition to earning bucks, you can earn special Swag Codes for additional points as well. It is easy to earn points that you can redeem for gift cards or prizes. For example, you can earn an Amazon.com e-gift card, Starbucks gift card, or PayPal gift card. When you refer friends, you earn Swag Bucks too!

Tips for maximizing your Swag Bucks earnings:

- Download one of the Swag Bucks browser plugins to earn for the searches you normally do.
- Follow @SwagBucks on Twitter for updates on new Swag Codes. (Enter these in the left-hand column on your Swag Bucks account page.)
- Read the Swag Bucks blog for updates on new features as well as info on Swag Codes.
- Shop through Swag Bucks to earn Swag Bucks on purchases.
- Refer your friends, and each time they earn points, so will you!

Another idea is to make coupons to give as gifts. Consider making a coupon for a free back rub, car wash, or dinner of their choice. These cost you nothing out of pocket and make great gifts. In addition to buying gifts, we enjoy giving handmade, home-canned goods or a service for many of the people on our list. One of the best gifts Melissa ever got was babysitting from a friend so that she and her husband could go out for a date. This gift cost no money but was so appreciated. You can always add an expiration date or funny exclusions to make the gift fun.

There are so many resources for finding freebies, samples, coupons, and special offers. Of course, we post all of the good ones that we find at StockpilingMoms.com. One problem with freebies is that they often don't last long. As always, when you request a freebie, know that there is no guarantee you will get it and always sign up with your junk email account. Here are a few places you can get some excellent freebies, coupons, and offers:

- BzzAgent.com
- VocalPoint.com
- KraftFirstTaste.com
- Freebies4Mom.com
- Facebook
- Twitter

We also love to give gifts from our stockpile. The following are two examples of how you can give gifts from your stockpile in style.

The first gift is a spa gift bag filled with bath lotions, bubbles, a towel wrap, slippers, high-end face creams, and so much more! The grand total out-of-pocket expense for the gift was $7! The value of the gift is well over $150! It is easy to collect items throughout the year at Rite Aid, CVS, and Walgreens, in addition to other sources such as BzzAgent.

The second gift idea is a Thirty One Thermal Tote filled with snacks. This gift was called "Snack Attack," and it had chips, snack mix, vitamin water, candy, and more! The out of pocket expense for this gift bag was less than $1! Melissa hosted a home party and earned the tote bag for free and then pulled everything out of her stockpile for the gift. The only expense was the gift wrap! It is amazing how you can think outside of the box and pull together gifts from your stockpile.

When it comes to gift wrap, be sure to be on the lookout for great deals. Always purchase your gift wrap items the day after Christmas at a discount or use coupons to get your gift wrap for the lowest out-of-pocket expense. For the past two years, we have been able to use coupons to get Hallmark gift wrap for less than $0.25 a roll. Also, consider reusing gift bags and boxes, eliminating gift bows, and thinking outside of the box when it comes to wrapping. Consider using newsprint and hand stamping it or using the funny papers.

In order to stockpile, you need a location to store your gifts. Melissa's husband built her a storage shelf, and Shelley uses an area in her stockpile room in her unfinished basement. You do need to keep in mind that you don't want children to have access to this storage or they may not be surprised at the holidays. Keeping your storage area secure is important. A great idea may be to swap with a friend and keep each other's gift-giving stockpile at the other's house.

You can also take advantage of gift card deals for yourself or others during the holidays. Many restaurants offer gift card deals like a free bonus gift card when you make a purchase. This is a great way to reduce your dining out budget. You do have to spend money out of pocket; however, you are typically getting a $10 bonus card, so by purchasing a gift card in advance for a favorite restaurant, you are able to dine out several times later in the year for free!

By utilizing your stockpile, you can give really useful gifts that your friends and family really enjoy getting, and it is easy on your budget because you're shopping from your stockpile instead of at the store! When it comes to groceries, we try our very best to stay out of the grocery stores around the holiday months. If you notice the ingredients you use will go on sale just prior to the holidays, stock up so you do not have to grocery shop during the rush of the season. Make a list of all the ingredients you will need for the holidays. You will probably be able to get them all before the full swing of the holidays start. This will allow you to enjoy the season.

If you are going to shop online, you should utilize cash back shopping. Cash back shopping allows you to earn cash back from your online purchases. The sites get a commission from the stores when you make a purchase, and instead of keeping that money, they share it with you. It is simple to earn cash back through these sites. As long as you login to your account and click through your links to shop, your purchases will result in you getting paid after you make a purchase.

Oftentimes you will get a signing bonus when you register, and in most cases, you earn money or credits when you refer people to sign up under you. It is a win-win situation. In addition, the sites offer you incentives or discounts to purchase through their site versus the retailer. Some cash back sites offer free shipping, discounts, coupons, special offers, or sales. These sites provide shoppers with the opportunity to earn cash back just by shopping at their favorite online stores. Cash back sites that we suggest include Ebates.com, ShopAtHome.com, and MrRebates.com. Other online resources for discount codes is retailmeknot.com, Savings.com, and CheapSally.com. Always check with these sites before you make a purchase online. It is a great way to save.

Don't overlook Black Friday. Shelley and her sister go out and shop every year on Black Friday. They enjoy the crowds, no sleep, shopping, extreme weather, and deals! Through her years of experience, Shelley has several strategies that make the Black Friday experience positive. Shelley suggests taking a chair for each person who is standing in line. This holds their spot if one person arrives early. When you are waiting in line, the people behind you often count to see where they are, and it is not fair if one person stands in line for twenty people. If you take five chairs that represent the five people who will be joining you, when someone is counting, they can see that there are five chairs and it is easy to see that the spot is taken for five people. Also, this saves your group's space, with no concern for room later.

Another tip is to make friends with those ahead of you in line. This is always a plus because who gets in first is who gets the offers first. Find out what they are planning to purchase and decide if it is worth your time to stay and wait in line. Stores often have very tight limits, and if there are only five of those items per store, which is often stated in the sales circular, then it might not be worth your time to stand in line.

Create a Black Friday Binder®. Include in the binder all of the sales circulars and a list of all of the coupons that match for each store circular. Shelley suggests placing them in a zippered pouch so that if you run across unadvertised deals, you have them handy. Include a small calculator and pen too! By creating a Black Friday Binder®, you will find that you are organized and will maximize your time. Print off store maps or outlet mall maps so that you are not wasting your time running from one store to another.

Check with your specific store location in advance to see if the store will let you shop versus check out at the exact time the sale starts. For example, Walmart allowed shoppers to shop before the sale time started, and they could check out at the exact time the sale started. This is a great place to send one of your "saved chair" people. Depending on the time frame, they may be able to shop while you wait and then come back to your location to shop again.

It is best to divide into groups and split your list. Consider driving in multiple cars. This way you can shop the sale and move on to save a place in the next line. Don't forget to utilize your chairs! If you have enough in your group, split up and wait at two stores; however, be sure to hold a spot for everyone with a chair. The number one Black Friday tip is don't forget to charge your cell phone. If you get separated and need to communicate, you will need a charged phone! Also, pack plenty of snacks, water, and warm beverages. Stopping for food can be a big budget buster. Best of all, have fun and enjoy!

12

what to do
with your savings

We believe in giving back to the community from our stockpile. We donate thousands of items every year to local charities and families in need. We go through our stockpile on the fifteenth of each month and decide what should be donated and what we will keep. At every class, someone will ask the question "What do you do with all that stuff and how can you possibly use it?" The answer is quite simple: if we can't, someone else will. We love to help people, and this is a great way to do it. At very little out-of-pocket expense, you are able to help someone in need. However, by inventorying your stockpile and planning monthly menus, you will find that you don't have much excess. We suggest purchasing a quantity to last your family based on what you use and need.

We also choose to donate when products are free. For example, we may buy dog food and treats when they are free and donate them to the animal shelter, or we may buy baby items and donate them to the Women's Crisis Center. Who can you give it to? You can go to Feeding America and find a local food bank. Also, in times of need such as natural disasters, giving from your stockpile is a great opportunity. By donating to the local Red Cross, you provide health and beauty aids and other necessities in a time of despair. Another opportunity to help is through Operation Christmas Child. Travel-size items and back-to-school supplies are perfect. Regardless of who you give to, it is a great opportunity for you to teach the gift of giving to your children and help others when giving financially may not be an option.

Another idea is to play "coupon fairy," Leaving behind coupons that are nearing expiration next to a product is a nice idea; just remember that some stores don't allow it because they don't like the mess on the shelves. Some stores provide a coupon bin for customers to exchange coupons with each other. This may be something to ask your local store manager about starting if they don't offer it. You may even volunteer to remove expired coupons for them. They could be donated to the military, as we will discuss next. Instead of playing coupon fairy, we often hand out coupons to shoppers who are purchasing a brand that we have a coupon for in our binder.

We want to share with you an awesome way to give back to those serving our country abroad! You can donate your expired coupons to be used by military families. They are allowed to use expired coupons six months to one year after the expiration date on base and at the commissaries abroad. The one thing that we hate to do is throw away an expired coupon, and now we never have to! For more information, visit www.ocpnet.org, www.couponstotroops .com, and also www.facebook.com/ExpiredCouponsForOverseas Military. Some American Legion Auxiliary groups also collect expired coupons. Check with your local American Legion Auxiliary to see if they participate. Please consider helping out our military by donating your coupons. It is just a small token of appreciation that we can provide to military families.

Now that you are saving hundreds of dollars a month, what are you going to do with your savings? For many of you, the money saved will go to pay debt. If you have not created your family budget, now would be a great time to do so. As we mentioned in chapter 7, creating a family budget will save your family money because you will be accountable for your spending. You will really be able to see where your money goes, and it will end up saving you money in the end.

We want to share with you how we use our savings so that you can see how you could use the money you save by stockpiling. Shelley brainstormed on what to do with her savings, and in the end, she decided the only way to make use of her savings was to save it. First, she and her family decided they would take what they saved from every shopping trip and divide it by four (the number of people in her family). The amount of money they save divided by four is put into a savings account. For instance, if she saves $247.95 at the store, she divides that by 4, which equals $61.98. She writes a check for $62 and places it into their "wish list" savings account. She feels that when you are saving so much at the store each week, you can afford to put something into savings.

She and her husband sat down and made a list of everything they wanted to purchase each year. Her wish list included chairs for her kitchen island, bedroom furniture, a new comforter and bed linens, and to have her bedroom and bathroom painted. Her husband's wish list consisted of a new garage cabinet for the kids' toys, a new workbench, and new shelves for the stockpile room. Next, they sat down with their lists and prioritized the items. They researched the best deals for each one and averaged a price out for each. When they have enough money saved from stockpiling to purchase an item on the list, they buy it. They will buy one item at a time. It is likely they will not buy them all in one year, which is why they call it their wish list. So Shelley's idea is that the next time you save a lot, save a little! Enjoy your stockpiling savings in a way that is best for you!

This idea can be used in many ways. You do not have to spend the money you save; you can save money for your child's college tuition, savings accounts, retirement, vacations, or whatever you choose. It is rewarding to know you did not have to take away from your family for things you "want"; instead, you can utilize the money you save from your stockpiling success.

After Melissa started stockpiling, she went from spending $450 to $500 a month to spending $130 a month on average. With this savings, she decided to start a "Disney fund." Each month she deposited $150 into the "Disney fund" account. As you know, going to Disney World is not cheap, so they decided saving and paying cash for the trip was the way to do it.

This is a great way to see your savings:

Date	Store	Retail	OOP	Total Savings	% Saved

Taking Your Dream Vacation

If you dream of taking your family to Disney World but think it is out of your reach, remember, you can do it! Melissa paid cash for her trip and plans to do it again! How did she do it? By skillfully using coupons and matching coupons to items on sale to pay cash for the Disney vacation. By banking the money from her budget each month that she "used" to spend on groceries, she was able to save without impacting the rest of her family budget. She deposited $150 from her "normal" grocery budget into her Disney fund each month. She and her family were very excited that they were able to save the money to pay cash for the Disney vacation in just two years. All that was possible by stockpiling.

After you make the decision to go to Disney World, *planning is key*. When it came time to plan the vacation, Melissa and her family priced the vacation through several avenues: through AAA, two authorized Disney travel agencies, and renting DVC points. In the end, the best price came from a travel agent. They made the decision to go during the off season for several reasons: it is less expensive, it is not as crowded, and it's cooler. In addition, Melissa scoured Disboards.com and found a code to use, which saved her 30 percent! Always look for a code before you book. The travel agent she booked through was able to use the code.

We wanted to share this with you because we tell people all of the time how stockpiling has changed our lives! If we did not stockpile, Melissa's family would not have been able to go on this dream vacation to Disney World by paying cash!

Decide if you are staying on Disney property or not. It is much less expensive to stay off property; however, we prefer to stay on property. We enjoy the benefits of Extra Magic Hours and the convenience. We also always choose to purchase the Disney Dining Plan. You cannot purchase the Dining Plan if you don't stay on property. We like to go to several Character Meals, and by choosing the Disney Dining Plan, there is no stress in how much those meals cost.

Next decide if you are driving or flying. Because of the increasing gas prices, Melissa made the decision to fly. Also, transportation to and from the airport is included as well as transportation within Disney World from parks, hotels, and Downtown Disney. If you won't need to rent a car, then flying may be less expensive than driving and may be a worthwhile choice for your budget.

Be sure to pack snacks or ship them to your hotel (if you are flying). We placed an order for drinks and snacks from Staples.com to arrive around the day of our arrival. Please be sure not to ship too far in advance though. Another idea if you are flying is to use the Garden Grocer (GardenGrocer.com). Pack a soft-side cooler to take bottled water or juice into the park. Pack snacks too. You will need them while you are waiting in lines, and it will save you money in the parks. You are allowed to take a soft-sided cooler into the park but not a rolling cooler or hard-side cooler. They do check your bags every time you enter the park; however, it is not a major inconvenience and is worth the savings. Another tip is to pack Crystal Light, Kool-Aid, or Propel packets with you so that you can add them to water. Water is free, and if you add one of these packets, you and your kids will enjoy a free drink over having to use a snack credit!

We suggest making a room request when booking your trip. Do your research on room locations—again, we suggest Disboards .com—after you select the resort you want to stay in. Things to consider are if you want a garden view or pool view, if you want to be near an elevator, what floor you want to be on, and if your family has any special needs.

Finally you want to map out your days. Decide if you are doing one park per day or if you are getting a park hopper. Because our son was young, we chose one park a day with a base ticket plan. However, in the future we will buy a park hopper to give us more freedom in planning. By choosing the one park a day option, you have to plan more because if you have the dining plan, you will want to make advanced reservations and you will need to know which parks you are going to each day. In addition, you will want to plan around Extra Magic Hours to take advantage of those too. Some people suggest avoiding Extra Magic Hours parks because they have a high crowd level, but we like to maximize our Extra Magic Hours. It is up to you.

We suggest that you buy a good stroller if you are taking a little one or rent one once you arrive. Also, buy a stroller organizer and a stroller rain cover. We suggest a stroller that is lightweight and folds easily. Another tip is to purchase cheap ponchos from the dollar store and package them in individual resealable bags so they are easy to hand out if necessary. Also, pack an umbrella or two. They are great for shade while walking around the park or standing to wait for a parade. Yes, someone will make a comment to you, but really, they are just wishing they had an umbrella to use on a hot day at the park.

Bring a couple of spray bottles with fans because they are $20 at the park. We like the ones in the park because they come with a neck strap, but we are not so fond of the price. You can find one similar at Walmart. One of Melissa's spray bottles was stolen from the seat of her stroller while she and her family ate lunch and parked the stroller outside. Her suggestion is to hide your fans because they are obviously "hot" items.

Be sure to take advantage of Extra Magic Hours if you are staying at one of the Walt Disney World resorts. The morning and evening Extra Magic Hours are worth it! Be at rope drop! You will get more done in that one hour than any other hour at the park. We planned what we were going to ride during Extra Magic Hours so we didn't waste any of our time. We also suggest enjoying your pool! Spend time there every day. We took a break around 2:00 almost every day. Most pools are open late too, which is nice after a long day at the parks.

A "Disney on a Dime" tip is to buy some small Disney souvenirs when they go on clearance at the Disney Store or at the Dollar Tree and take them with you. Another great place to find Disney items is in the dollar bins at Michael's and Target. We purchased small stuffed Mickeys for around $3.99 at the Disney store, and "Tinkerbell" left these for the kids on our first night, along with a little "pixie dust," or glitter. We purchased a few other items that we gave the kids instead of purchasing expensive items at the park. We also gave each child a budgeted amount of spending money, and when it was gone, it was gone. Another affordable souvenir is the pressed pennies. They are available everywhere. Bring a roll of pennies and quarters for lots of inexpensive fun!

Bring washcloths or bandannas to wet and put on your neck when you are hot. This is a great tip that Melissa's friend Kristy gave her, and it works like a charm. Bring in a small first aid kit with you. They do have a couple of first aid stations that may or may not be conveniently located to where you need them. Pack wet wipes and hand sanitizer—you will need them!

If you purchase the Disney Dining Plan and have a child on the dining plan, they do not keep track of children's versus adult meals for the Quick Service Plan. So you can get adult meals for all of your Quick Service meals. You can share a meal as well and then "bank" your meals to be used later. If you have leftover "snacks," they can be used at the candy shops for souvenirs to take home! Make advanced reservations for character meals. It is the best way to see the characters and avoid standing in line waiting for them in the park. If your child has a favorite character or two, schedule them quickly (you can book 180 days in advance) because they book up. You will not have to wait in line to see the characters and can enjoy more attractions. If you schedule early breakfasts at the parks, you get into the park before the general public. This is especially nice at Animal Kingdom and Epcot.

We suggest visiting Downtown Disney. We really enjoyed it,

and there is a nice spray area for the kids to play in that you will want to take advantage of. There is also one at almost most every park, and it makes for a great place to cool down. We suggest going in the afternoon or for a late lunch or early dinner to avoid the crowds. Have your children wear their bathing suits under their clothes or bring a change of clothing. Always carry bathing suits for the children at Disney World.

Be sure to give yourself at least one hour each way for bus transportation. Take the ferry and the monorail. We suggest taking every single mode of transportation that you can! We enjoyed seeing how many modes of transportation we could take in one week! Use the fast passes. They are great! See shows and parades and the 3-D movies. Map and plan out what you are going to do each day or you will waste your time once you get to the park. Planning your trip is the key to success!

Take advantage of Ride Switch if you have a little one. This is an awesome use of your fast pass because after your other family members ride, you can ride and take someone with you. If you have a little boy or little girl, we suggest doing the Bibbidi-Bobbidi-Boutique. It is the best money we spent on the trip. It is approximately $50 for the princess makeover (pack your own gown), and the cool dude makeover is only $7. You could also get a cut or style at the barber shop in Magic Kingdom, which is very affordable and makes your child feel special.

Create your own autograph book using a photo book you get on sale. We opted to buy a spiral bound index card book to use. The children used this to collect signatures, and then we put them into a photo album with pictures of the kids with the characters once we got home. We also bought an 8x10 photo mat from Michael's (using a 40 percent off coupon), and we had the princesses sign that. We put it into a resealable bag and slipped it into a backpack. The characters really liked signing it, and it made them feel special. As a result, they normally spent a little more one on one time talking to our kids. Bring sharpie markers for the characters because they need a wide pen to write with.

Bring your own glow sticks! They are very expensive at Disney World, and you can pick them up at the Dollar Tree or after

Halloween on clearance and save money and time purchasing them there. They even have swords, necklaces, bracelets, and more. This is a huge money saver. Our favorite sites for Disney research include www.disboards.com, www.mousesavers.com, www.allears.net, and www.wdwinsiders.com.

reader testimonials

We also want to share with you several reader testimonials that we have received. There is nothing more exciting than to see how stockpiling has impacted one of our readers.

"About eight months after my husband lost his job, I took Melissa's Couponing 101 class. As a stay-at-home mother of three, I was interested to learn how I could save money and be more frugal with our family's tight budget. I was *amazed* at what I learned and eagerly started putting Melissa's couponing strategies to work. I saved all of my receipts and would calculate my savings each month. I often saved as much as $250 per month and began to accumulate a very nice stockpile that I paid surprising little for! During my first year of "couponing," I saved a total of $2,400! I am currently in my second year of frugal savings and am delighted at what a significant difference it has made for our family! Thanks, Stockpiling Moms!"

—*Elisabeth Skeese*

"Why pay for toothpaste when you can always get it free? I have always known that coupons would save my family money, but I was never aware of just how much. We have four children in our family, and our monthly grocery bill was outrageous. We were living paycheck to paycheck and would often be out of the essentials the day before payday. After being frustrated each week, I decided to explore coupons. I continued getting page suggestions for coupon saving sites, so I decided to accept one and explore my options.

"Let me just say, WOW! It amazed me how many items I had been paying full price for what my family uses on a regular basis. During the summer 2010, I read articles about Couponing and Stockpiling 101 and decided I was going to give it a try. I spent three hours my first week planning and locating coupons. I had over ninety coupons to use for that grocery trip. I felt so empowered to walk into the store knowing I basically had $90 in my pocket. That is exactly what coupons are—money! Since last summer, I spend an average of two to three hours each week planning my savings. I have saved my family over $3,000 in eight months just by using coupons and knowing how to stack them to get the best deal available. If someone said you would get a $450 paycheck each month for approximately ten to twelve hours of work, wouldn't you accept the offer?

"The most important thing I have learned throughout my couponing experience is that I had to find what worked for my family. We don't have much room to store items we want to stockpile, so I only buy perishables that we can use within three to six months and health and beauty items to last nine to twelve months. I challenge you to take some time out of your busy schedule this week and explore the benefits of coupons. I can guarantee you will be extremely hesitant to ever buy a product again without a coupon. Best of luck with your couponing journey!"

—*Erica*

"I love your site. I use it ALL the time. I have saved so much money over the last two years! I tell everyone in the grocery store when they ask how do you do it, 'Go to StockpilingMoms. End of story! That is your one-stop shop to savings. They don't have you running all over the Internet to look; they post matchups for you.' StockpilingMoms has become my shopping go-to site. I love the matchups! This site has saved my family thousands of dollars! I tell everyone that stops me at the stores about StockpilingMoms! Shelley and Melissa really know their stuff. They give you the knowledge and skills to make coupons work for you. No more leaving the store with coupons in my pocket! I truly have the confidence to know and tell cashiers when a price has rung up wrong! I know it's my money, and I want to buy and save as much as possible, and this site helps with all of this!"

—*Deirdre*

"I just wanted to let you know that I went to Kroger after viewing your matchups, and I saved 51 percent! You guys make it so easy to save money! Thank you so much!"

—*Rachel*

"In a world where technological advancements occur daily and blogs are a dime a dozen, StockpilingMoms goes above and beyond to keep their readers loyal and interested by keeping up-to-date on all that is current! As moms themselves, they know that time and money are the two things that most families do not have enough of. And they fuel their site with that concept in mind! Stockpiling Moms.com is the easiest site to use. Their store matchups are broken down by the product, the sale price, the coupon needed, along with where to find that coupon (which is *amazing*!), and then finally the price you will pay when you use the coupon on that product! It is so easy!

"You can choose the store that you shop at and look at what that store is offering for the week, or if you are really limited on your time, you can just go to the section with the Hot Deals. This will actually break down the week's top deals and steals so you are sure not to miss the best of the best!

"StockpilingMoms has helped cut my family's grocery budget by more than half, with not a lot of time invested weekly! As a mom of three children myself, this is enough to keep me coming back! They offer really neat features that make it so easy and convenient to use that it would not be beneficial for you to go to another website. StockpilingMoms even has links on the site that will take you directly to the website needed to get the online coupons. And if you happen to have a little extra time and want to have some fun, they have recipes, frugal tips, and even a section with giveaways. And when I say giveaways, I don't mean extra things that they have accumulated over time—they always have up-to-date and desired giveaways!

"I will continue to use StockpilingMoms simply because it is a no-brainer—saving money with very minimal time invested leaves me more time to spend with my family!"

—*Jamie York*

GLOSSARY

basic coupon lingo

This is some basic coupon lingo that will help you on your journey to stockpiling. These are common abbreviations in the coupon world. It is important to understand this lingo so that you can get the biggest bang for your buck while shopping. This is a list that you should refer back to often in understanding how to strategically use coupons.

BOGO—Buy One Get One Free coupon or offer

B2GO—Buy 2 Get One Free coupon or offer

Blinkie—Coupon machine at the grocery store with a red blinking light on it. Coupons that come from the machines are also referred to as blinkies.

Bricks—"Bricks" coupons are Internet printable coupons. If you print a "bricks" coupon, you will know based on the Bricks URL and a picture of a computer or printer with a small blinking dot as it sends the information to your printer.

Cat—Manufacturer coupon that prints from a Catalina machine at the cash register. A Catalina machine is a marketing tool that manufacturers use to print coupons as incentives to shop.

Coupon policy—Each store has a coupon policy. The policy stipulates what their procedure is in regard to using coupons. It is important to know that policies change often and can vary from store to store at the manager's discretion. Some policies are corporate policies and some vary by store. It is important to contact the store you shop at and find out their coupon policy before you shop.

Dead—Refers to a dead deal, or that an offer is no longer valid. This is often used in terms of a coupon that runs out of prints.

DND—Do Not Double. In reference to coupons. Some manufacturers place a DND at the top of the coupon by the expiration date, meaning that the coupon should not be doubled at the store.

Double—A coupon that the store doubles the face value of, if the coupon policy is to double coupons.

ECB—Extra Care Buck (CVS)

EX or Exp.—Expires or Expiration Date, in reference to coupons or rebates

GM—General Mills coupon insert, found in the Sunday paper

HBA—Health & Beauty Aids, in reference to products at the store

Hot—Hot Deal or Coupon, a deal or coupon that will not last long

Inserts—Coupons found in the Sunday paper

IP—Internet Printable coupon, a coupon that you can print online

IVC—Instant Value Coupons (Walgreens)

Manager's discretion—A store manager often has the ability to set limits on coupons used and items purchased.

MQ—Manufacturer Coupon, provided by the manufacturer to use when making a purchase

MIR—Mail-in Rebate, provided by the manufacturer to use when making a purchase. You will pay out of pocket and receive a rebate in the form of a check back from the manufacturer.

NED—No Expiration Date, a coupon that has no expiration date.

NT WT—Net Weight, in reference to coupons that stipulate based on the wording that you must purchase a product with a specific net weight.

OOP—Out of Pocket. This is the total that you pay, or your total expense.

OOS—Out of Stock, when an item is not available to purchase

OTC—Over-the-counter medication, in reference to products at the store that do not require a prescription.

OYNO—On Your Next Order. This is an incentive where you make a qualifying purchase and then receive an incentive to use on your next purchase.

P&G—Proctor & Gamble coupon insert, found in the Sunday paper

Peelie—Coupon found attached to a product. You have to peel it off to use it. It comes from the manufacturer attached to the product to use when you make that purchase.

POP—Proof of purchase, used when submitting an MIR.

Q—Coupon, the same as cash

QQ—Coupon Queen, a person who uses coupons to stockpile or save big

RC—Rain Check, obtained when an item is OOS. You can extend the price of the sale when you obtain a rain check from the store. Not all stores write rain checks.

RP—Red Plum coupon insert, found in the Sunday paper (formerly called Valassis)

RR—Register Reward (Walgreens). This is a manufacturer coupon and is an incentive from the manufacturer to make a qualifying purchase.

Run—Going to the store to use your coupons

SCR—Single Check Rebate (Rite Aid), an incentive program that offers you MIRs when you make qualifying purchases.

SPM—Stockpiling Moms

SS—Smart Source coupon insert, found in the Sunday paper

Stacking—Using one manufacturer coupon and one store coupon on the same product (if store coupon policy allows)

Stockpile—A pile or storage location for bulk materials, including groceries, personal care products, or household products

Tearpad—A pad found hanging from a store shelf or display. This could have either coupons or MIRs.

Triple—A coupon that the store triples the face value of, if the coupon policy is to triple coupons.

UPR—+UP Rewards (Rite Aid)

UPC—Universal Product Code. Barcode on the product, used for MIRs.

Wellness+—Store loyalty card at Rite Aid

WYB—When You Buy, the wording on a coupon. See next section for more information.

YMMV—Your Mileage May Vary. That is, this deal worked for me, but it may not work for you.

Coupon Phrases to Know:

Get this free when you buy that: If the coupon says "get this free when you buy (WYB) that," you can use one coupon for the "that," and the WYB will be for the "this" item.

One per customer: To purchase multiples, you will need to take a family member along with you. Each one of you is considered a customer.

One per household: You are limited to one per household/address.

One per purchase: You can use one coupon for every item that you purchase unless the coupon reads "save $2 on 2," and then you would have to purchase two items to use the coupon.

One per transaction: This means you can use only one coupon for the transaction, which is all combined items paid for at the same time. You can put the bar down and break your order into multiple transactions.

One per visit: You can buy only one per trip; however, leaving the store and coming back in counts.

10/10: Many stores are now offering 10 for 10 specials. You do not have to purchase 10 of the same item or even 10 items total to qualify for the $1 per item pricing.

Author photos by Amanda Greenwell.
http://www.amandagreenwellphotography.com/

about the authors

In 2009, Melissa Jennings and Shelley King founded Stock-pilingMoms.com and made it their mission to save money for their families. They share their journey to savvy living as they use coupons to build their stockpile and live a debt-free life. Melissa and Shelley are best friends who met through International Adoption.

Melissa taught family and consumer science (home economics) on the high school level for eleven years and holds a masters degree in education. Shelley spent three years as a substance abuse counselor, educating people and giving them the tools to aid them in living a healthy lifestyle. Melissa and Shelley are stockpiling experts who want to help you stretch your family budget. Melissa has one son (Peyton), and Shelley has two boys (Chase and Caleb), all of whom were born in Guatemala.

exclusive coupon

coupon clutch

Receive

10% off

when you use the code

STOCKPILINGBOOK

at http://www.couponclutch.com/stockpiling